Full Speed Ahead in Reading

Reproducible Activity Sheets for Grades 4-6

Troll Associates

Troll Teacher Time Savers provide a quick source of self-contained lessons and practice material, designed to be used as full-scale lessons or to make productive use of those precious extra minutes that sometimes turn up in the day's schedule.

Troll Teacher Time Savers can help you to prepare a made-to-order program for your students. Select the sequence of Time Savers that will meet your students' needs, and make as many photocopies of each page as you require. Since Time Savers include progressive levels of complexity and difficulty in each book, it is possible to individualize instruction, matching the needs of each student.

Those who need extra practice and reinforcement for catching up in their skills can benefit from Troll Teacher Time Savers, while other students can use Time Savers for enrichment or as a refresher for skills in which they haven't had recent practice. Time Savers can also be used to diagnose a student's knowledge and skills level, in order to see where extra practice is needed.

Time Savers can be used as homework assignments, classroom or small-group activities, shared learning with partners, or practice for standardized testing. See "Answer Key & Skills Index" to find the specific skill featured in each activity.

Pages 1-42 introduce and reinforce the following skills: finding the main idea, selecting the topic, determining the details, making inferences and drawing conclusions, and using context clues. Generally, question #1 is a main idea or topic question; #2 and #3 focus on details; #4 is an inference or drawing conclusion question; #5 is a context clue question.

Pages 43-50 focus more specifically on the skills of making inferences and drawing conclusions. They can be used while working on pages 1-42, or before or after any of these pages.

Pages 51-72 deal with distinguishing cause from effect or fact from opinion, and determining tone.

Pages 73 and 74 are overall review pages of all of the skills.

ANSWER KEY & SKILLS INDEX

Page 1, **Tadpole Story:** 1-c; 2-c; 3-c; 4-a; 5-c. **(topic, details, inference, context clues)**

Page 2, **A Room at the Top:** 1-Answers will vary; 2-three; 3-round; 4-Answers will vary; 5-a large sofa. **(main idea, details, drawing conclusions, synonyms)**

Page 3, **Mistaken Identity:** 1-b; 2-b; 3-a; 4-a; 5-b. **(topic, details, inference, context clues)**

Page 4, **Sylvester:** 1-Sylvester is smart; 2-out of gas; 3-Christopher Lee's; 4-Answers will vary; 5-competitors or challengers. **(main idea, details, drawing conclusions, context clues)**

Page 5, **Friends in Nature:** 1-b; 2-a; 3-a; 4-b; 5-c. **(topic, details, inference, context clues)**

Page 6, **Nicky & the Musical Mice:** 1-last sentence; 2-at least two; 3-an hour; 4-Answers will vary; 5-a large group of people crowded together. **(main idea, details, drawing conclusions, context clues)**

Page 7, **Starfish:** 1-a; 2-b; 3-c; 4-a; 5-c. **(topic, details, inference, context clues)**

Page 8, **Let Your Hair Down:** 1-But no one in history ever had hair that was longer than Rapunzel's; 2-2 bottles; 3-all afternoon; 4-patience, It took a long time to comb her hair but she kept at it until she was finished; 5-kept within bounds, restricted, or imprisoned. **(main idea, details, drawing conclusions, context clues)**

Page 9, **Talk to the Animals:** 1-b; 2-c; 3-c; 4-a; 5-b. **(main idea, details, inference, context clues)**

Page 10, **Unfortunate Felix:** 1-c) Felix is always in trouble; 2-because he threw food in the lunchroom; 3-math; 4-Answers will vary; 5-a period of time in which a person is kept or detained. **(main idea, details, drawing conclusions, context clues)**

Page 11, **The Mysterious Monarchs:** 1-c; 2-b; 3-a; 4-c; 5-a. **(topic, details, inference, context clues)**

Page 12, **A Circus Dream:** 1-the first sentence; 2-big red nose, polka-dot suit; 3-ten; 4-no, Explanations will vary; 5-a large, thick-skinned mammal, like an elephant. **(main idea, details, drawing conclusions, context clues)**

Page 13, **Unusual Animals:** 1-b; 2-c; 3-c; 4-a; 5-a. **(topic, details, inference, context clues)**

Page 14, **The Country Fair:** 1-Of all the animals he saw at the fair, Horace liked the dogs best; 2-at the country fair; 3-dogs barked when he came into view/ wagged their tails when he came near/ licked his face when he stopped to say hello/ sat still when being patted, rubbed, and chucked; 4-Answers will vary; 5-gave an affectionate, playful pat under the chin. **(topic sentence, details, drawing conclusions, context clues)**

Page 15, **A Bear From China:** 1-b; 2-c; 3-b; 4-a; 5-b. **(topic, details, inference, context clues)**

Page 16, **Julie Goes Shopping:** 1-c)The Biggest Pumpkin; 2-3; 3-Peterson's Pumpkin Farm; 4-She didn't find a big enough pumpkin there; 5-of a small size. **(topic, details, drawing conclusions, context clues)**

Page 17, **Animal Camouflage:** 1-b; 2-c; 3-c; 4-b; 5-b. **(topic, details, inference, context clues)**

Page 18, **A Mountain Meadow:** 1-Spring had finally arrived; 2-sun shined more brightly/ snow melted/ grass was growing again/ buds appeared on trees/ robins had arrived/ first flower was in bloom; 3-into the branches of an evergreen tree; 4-building a nest; 5-a small brook or stream. **(main idea, details, drawing conclusions, context clues)**

Page 19, **The Largest Seal:** 1-c; 2-b; 3-c; 4-c; 5-b. **(topic, details, inference, drawing conclusions)**

Page 20, **Twinkle Toes:** 1-Fran was the best dancer in the state; 2-Myrna; 3-Each had graduated at the top of his or her class; 4-no, Flo was the best dancer on her block, yet Fran could dance better; 5-a contest of skill for profit, prize, or position. **(main idea, details, drawing conclusions, context clues)**

Page 21, **Sweet Treats:** 1-b; 2-c; 3-c; 4-c; 5-b. **(topic, details, inference, context clues)**

Page 22, **The Mysterious Neighbor:** 1-first sentence; 2-high wall, iron gate, guard; 3-Jeeves; 4-c) Ms. Simoleon was very rich; 5-left, retreated, departed, disappeared. **(main idea, details, drawing conclusions, synonyms)**

Page 23, **What Are Dreams?:** 1-b; 2-c; 3-b; 4-a; 5-b. **(topic, details, inference, context clues)**

Page 24, **Good Grief, Gus!:** 1-Gus has a big appetite; 2-pork chops or hamburgers or hot dogs; 3-cookies and ice cream; 4-Answers will vary; 5-eats, devours. **(topic sentence, details, drawing conclusions, synonyms)**

Page 25, **A Folk Hero:** 1-b; 2-c; 3-c; 4-c; 5-b. **(topic, details, inference, context clues)**

Page 26, **A Strange Thing:** 1-Answers will vary; 2-gumdrops/ hard candies/ marshmallows/ candy corn/ jellybeans/ chocolate bars/ peanut brittle; 3-peanut brittle; 4-d) Lana is thoughtful. Explanations will vary; 5-a sweet, such as candy. **(topic, details, drawing conclusions, context clues)**

Page 27, **Fight or Flight:** 1-c; 2-b; 3-a; 4-a; 5-a. **(topic, details, inference, context clues)**

Page 28, **Jeffrey's Surprise:** 1-b) Jeffrey changed a lot over the summer vacation; 2-unfriendly, impolite, selfish; 3-Mr. Green; 4-Answers will vary; 5-rude, not courteous. **(main idea, details, drawing conclusions, context clues)**

Page 29, **Strange Plants:** 1-c; 2-b; 3-c; 4-c; 5-a. **(topic, details, inference, context clues)**

Page 30, **A Big Secret:** 1-No one knew the secret formula except Sheldon Soyburger; 2-Tess; 3-She squirted super sauce on every burger; 4-probably named for the inventor of the super sauce, Sheldon Soyburger, or because the shop sells soyburgers; 5-a flat pan used for cooking. **(main idea, details, drawing conclusions, context clues)**

Page 31, **Stones of Mystery:** 1-c; 2-b; 3-b; 4-b; 5-a. **(topic, details, inference, context clues)**

Page 32, **A Sweet Tale:** 1-c) Louise couldn't decide what kind of candy to buy; 2-in a big glass case; 3-chocolate-covered cherries; 4-Answers will vary; 5-questioned, asked. **(main idea, details, drawing conclusions, context clues)**

Page 33, **Rough Riders:** 1-c; 2-b; 3-b; 4-c; 5-a. **(main idea, details, inference, context clues)**

Page 34, **Vacation Blues:** 1-a) A storm was coming; 2-change in the direction of the breeze/ cooler/ ocean less calm/ whitecaps/ angrier waves/ gusts of wind/ dark clouds; 3-west; 4-probably leave the beach and head for shelter; 5-struck against. **(main idea, details, prediction, context clues)**

Page 35, **Let's Ride:** 1-b; 2-c; 3-a; 4-c; 5-b. **(topic, details, inference, context clues)**

Page 36, **Write It Right!:** 1-But Fritz never made mistakes; 2-He thought about what he was going to write about; 3-He proofread his paper; 4-Answers will vary; 5-dictionary. **(main idea, details, drawing conclusions, synonyms)**

Page 37, **Dribble & Shoot:** 1-b; 2-c; 3-c; 4-a; 5-b. **(topic, details, inference, context clues)**

Page 38, **Summer Fun:** 1-Answers will vary; 2-in the front yard; 3-50 cents; 4-They would be very hot and thirsty; 5-something added or required to form a mixture/ element, component. **(main idea, details, drawing conclusions, context clues and synonyms)**

Page 39, **The New Athletes:** 1-b; 2-b; 3-a; 4-a; 5-a. **(topic, details, inference, context clues)**

Page 40, **Report Card Day:** 1-Everyone had received good grades except Zeke; 2-Barney & Bill; 3-Charley; 4-b) Charley liked to tease Charlotte; 5-gloomy, fretful/ Answers will vary. **(main idea, details, inference, synonyms and word usage)**

Page 41, **Lobster Parade:** 1-c; 2-c; 3-a; 4-b; 5-a.
(topic, details, inference, context clues)

Page 42, **Life in Space:** 1-Answers will vary; 2-since at least the 5th century B.C.; 3-radio telescopes; 4-b) intelligent life on another planet; 5-someone who lives in a place, a resident.
(main idea, details, inference, context clues)

Page 43, **Introducing Inference:** 1-e; 2-h; 3-l; 4-r; 5-k; 6-j; 7-f; 8-o; 9-b; 10-n; 11-s; 12-a; 13-p; 14-c; 15-q; 16-d; 17-t; 18-i; 19-m; 20-g. **(inference)**

Page 44, **Working With Inference:** 1-g; 2-j; 3-c; 4-o; 5-b; 6-q; 7-t; 8-p; 9-e; 10-r; 11-i; 12-h; 13-a; 14-s; 15-l; 16-d; 17-n; 18-m; 19-k; 20-f. **(inference)**

Page 45, **Inference—A Review:** 1-c; 2-c; 3-a; 4-c; 5-c. **(inference)**

Page 46, **Learning to Draw Conclusions:** 1-c; 2-b; 3-c; 4-a; 5-c; 6-a; 7-b; 8-b. **(drawing conclusions)**

Page 47, **Drawing Conclusions:** 1-c; 2-b; 3-a; 4-c; 5-c; 6-c; 7-b; 8-b. **(drawing conclusions)**

Page 48, **Practice Drawing Conclusions:** 1-b; 2-c; 3-b; 4-a; 5-b; 6-b; 7-c; 8-b. **(drawing conclusions)**

Page 49, **Reviewing Inference & Drawing Conclusions:** 2-grocer; 3-auto mechanic; 4-lawyer; 5-architect; 6-doctor; 7-waiter/waitress; 8-teacher; 9-plumber; 10-secretary; 11-nurse; 12-politician; 13-dentist; 14-insurance agent; 15-newscaster; 16-electrician; 17-police officer; 18-salesperson; 19-weathercaster. **(inference, drawing conclusions)**

Page 50, **Inference & Drawing Conclusions—A Review:** 1-true; 2-false; 3-true; 4-false; 5-false; 6-false. 1-false; 2-false; 3-true; 4-false; 5-true; 6-false; 7-true. **(inference, drawing conclusions)**

Page 51, **Matching Cause & Effect:** 1-f; 2-h; 3-d; 4-k; 5-b; 6-l; 7-j; 8-m; 9-c; 10-n; 11-o; 12-i; 13-g; 14-a; 15-e. **(cause & effect)**

Page 52, **Signal Words—Cause & Effect:** 1-If/then; 2-so that; 3-because; 4-consequently; 5-Since; 6-in order that; 7-resulted; 8-has caused; 9-has caused; 10-Since. **(cause & effect)**

Page 53, **Cause & Effect Statements:** 1-because; 2-In order that; 3-so that; 4-resulted; 5-because; 6-consequently; 7-because; 8-If/then; 9-Because; 10-As a result. **(cause & effect)**

Page 54, **Finding the Cause:** 1-Because televisions were so expensive at first; 2-because they were so exciting; 3-since people could watch TV at home; 4-when they get sick; 5-Medicine is a highly skilled practice; 6-If you need an operation; 7-because hospitals are so expensive; 8-Because most people get sick at some time; 9-because of aerial bombing; 10-As you grow older. **(cause)**

Page 55, **Locating Cause & Effect:** 1-E/C; 2-C/E; 3-C/E; 4-E/C; 5-E/C; 6-C/E. **(cause & effect)**

Page 56, **Cause & Effect in a Passage:** 1-a.It means making so many decisions all the time/ b.It is a contact sport/ c.It is colorful; 2-In both games the players stop after each move (play) to decide on the next one; 3-Effect: Football is popular/ Cause: because there are so many reasons for liking it; 4-Effect: Half times are popular/ Cause: because marching bands are fun to watch; 5-Effect: the rough action of football is exciting/ Cause: because it tests the players. **(cause & effect)**

Page 57, **Finding Cause & Effect:** 1-Cause: Because planes are so fast/ Effect: people can now cross the United States in about five hours; 2-Effect: Traveling is faster than ever today/ Cause: because a plane can fly at about 600 miles per hour; 3-Cause: Because people can get places so fast/ Effect: they can go longer distances on their vacations; 4-Effect: Planes themselves have been getting faster all the time/ Cause: as a result of advancing technology; 5-Effect: Now people can go from New York to Paris in about 3 1/2 hours/ Cause: because of the supersonic Concorde. **(cause & effect)**

Page 58, **Fact & Opinion:** 2-opinion; 3-fact; 4-opinion; 5-fact; 6-opinion; 7-opinion; 8-fact; 9-opinion; 10-opinion; 11-fact; 12-opinion; 13-fact; 14-opinion; 15-opinion. **(fact & opinion)**

Page 59, **Distinguishing Fact From Opinion:** 2-fact; 3-opinion; 4-opinion; 5-opinion; 6-fact; 7-opinion; 8-fact; 9-opinion; 10-fact; 11-fact; 12-fact; 13-opinion; 14-fact; 15-opinion. **(fact & opinion)**

Page 60, **Fact & Opinion Game:** 1-X; 2-X; 3-O; 4-X; 5-X; 6-O; 7-O; 8-O; 9-X. **(fact & opinion)**

Page 61, **Fun With Fact & Opinion:** 1-O; 2-X; 3-X; 4-O; 5-O; 6-X; 7-O; 8-O; 9-X. **(fact & opinion)**

Page 62, **Choosing the Facts:** 2-first sentence; 3-first sentence; 4-first sentence; 5-second sentence; 6-first sentence; 7-second sentence; 8-second sentence; 9-second sentence. **(fact)**

Page 63, **Recognizing an Opinion:** 2-first sentence; 3-second sentence; 4-second sentence; 5-first sentence; 6-second sentence; 7-first sentence; 8-first sentence. **(opinion)**

Page 64, **Finding the Fact:** 1-second sentence; 2-second sentence; 3-second sentence; 4-second sentence; 5-second sentence; 6-second sentence; 7-first sentence; 8-second sentence. **(fact)**

Page 65, **Locating Fact & Opinion:** First paragraph: 1-O; 2-F; 3-F; 4-F; 5-O; 6-O; 7-F; 8-F; 9-F; 10-F; Second paragraph: 1-F; 2-O; 3-F; 4-F; 5-F; 6-O; 7-F; 8-F; 9-F; 10-O. **(fact & opinion)**

Page 66, **Reading a Graph—Fact & Opinion:** 1-F; 2-F; 3-O; 4-O; 5-F; 6-O; 7-O; 8-O; 9-O; 10-F. **(fact & opinion)**

Page 67, **Separating Fact From Opinion:** O, F, F, O, F, O, F, F, F, F, O, F, F, F, F. **(fact & opinion)**

Page 68, **Is It Fact or Opinion?:** O, O, F, O, F, F, O, F, O, F, O, O, F. **(fact & opinion)**

Page 69, **Understanding Tone:** 2-minus; 3-plus; 4-minus; 5-minus; 6-plus; 7-plus; 8-minus; 9-plus; 10-minus; 11-plus; 12-plus; 13-minus; 14-plus; 15-minus. **(tone)**

Page 70, **Working With Tone:** 2-plus; 3-minus; 4-minus; 5-minus; 6-plus; 7-plus; 8-plus; 9-minus; 10-plus; 11-plus; 12-minus; 13-minus; 14-plus; 15-minus. **(tone)**

Page 71, **Tone—Judgment Words:** First paragraph-C. praise; Second paragraph-A. sarcasm, B. dislike. **(tone)**

Page 72, **Tone—A Review:** First section-great job, meet all kinds of people, fun, interesting, few of them are dishonest, get to know all the different parts of the city, beautiful, unusual, exciting, very rewarding experience, Answers may vary; Second section-one of the most popular vacation spots, great, spectacular, luxurious, spacious, Answers may vary; Third section-calm, relaxed, small, pleasant, one-horse, some kind of prize, all two of them, dreary food, one theater, five-year-old movies, Answers may vary. **(tone)**

Page 73, **Time to Review:** 1-O, F, F, O; 2-c; 3-b; 4-b; 5-scenic, marvelous, crystal lake, rolling woodland, varied range of opportunities, a. **(review)**

Page 74, **Overall Review:** 1-O, O, F, F; 2-E/C; 3-c; 4-d; 5-absolutely delightful, sings like a nightingale, graceful as a gazelle, some problems, need to take voice lessons, occasional sour note, flawless, enjoyable, a. **(review)**

Tadpole Story

Read the story. Then circle the correct answer to each question.

When tadpoles hatch from frogs' eggs, they look like little fish. They live in the water and breath through gills, like fish. A tadpole has no neck—its round head is connected to its body in such a way that it is difficult to tell the two apart. It uses its long tail to swim in the water.

The tadpole is always changing. First the tadpole's head starts to take shape. After a while it grows back legs, then front legs. Its tail becomes shorter and shorter. Just before it turns into a frog, it loses its gills. Now it can live out of the water. It almost looks like a frog except for its short tail. Soon the animal <u>absorbs</u> its tail and is an adult frog.

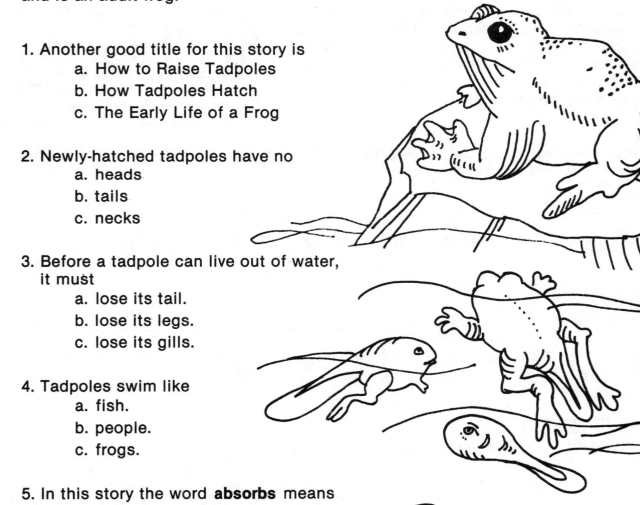

1. Another good title for this story is
    a. How to Raise Tadpoles
    b. How Tadpoles Hatch
    c. The Early Life of a Frog

2. Newly-hatched tadpoles have no
    a. heads
    b. tails
    c. necks

3. Before a tadpole can live out of water, it must
    a. lose its tail.
    b. lose its legs.
    c. lose its gills.

4. Tadpoles swim like
    a. fish.
    b. people.
    c. frogs.

5. In this story the word **absorbs** means
    a. sees.
    b. pays attention to.
    c. takes it into its body.

Name_____ Date _____

A Room at the Top

Read the paragraph. Then answer the questions.

Felicia's favorite place was at one end of the attic of her grandmother's house. Nobody else ever went there. But Felicia went there every chance she got. She didn't mind that she had to climb up three long flights of stairs. She didn't mind the creaking sound the attic door made when it opened. And she didn't mind having to squeeze between a stack of old papers and a musty old trunk. Because at the far end of the attic was a small room that was empty except for a big, worn-out, old <u>davenport</u>. It had overstuffed cushions and thick, soft armrests. When Felicia sat on it, she could look out a tiny, round window in the attic wall and see almost all the way down Main Street. She would sit there for hours and look out that window. There was no other place she liked as much.

1. Think about the main idea of the story—what the story is mainly about. Then use that main idea to help you think up a new title for the story.

   _____

2. How many flights of stairs did Felicia have to climb to reach her favorite place?

   _____

3. What shape was the window? _____

4. How do you think Felicia would have felt if her grandmother moved to a different house in the same town?

   _____

5. Can you think of another word for *davenport*? Write it here. _____

   _____

Mistaken Identity

Read the story. Then circle the correct answer to each question.

A dolphin is a sea mammal, not a fish. Dolphins live in the water and breathe air. They breathe through a blowhole on top of their heads when they swim to the surface of the water. When dolphins are underwater, their blowholes close so that no water gets in.

Dolphins are small whales. Many people use the names "dolphin" and "porpoise" interchangeably. But they are not the same. Porpoises belong to a different group in the whale family. Most porpoises that entertain at aquariums are really bottle-nosed dolphins. These intelligent animals can be trained to do all kinds of tricks. Some even make up their own games! Scientists think that dolphins are among the most intelligent of all animals. They hope, someday, to be able to communicate with them.

1. Think about the story. What is it mostly about? Pick a good title.
   - a. Animal Tricks
   - b. Dolphins and Porpoises
   - c. Breathing Underwater

2. The dolphin is a small kind of
   - a. fish.
   - b. whale.
   - c. porpoise.

3. Dolphins learn to do tricks because they are
   - a. intelligent.
   - b. playful.
   - c. mammals.

4. From the story you can tell that whales are
   - a. not fish.
   - b. smaller than dolphins.
   - c. not intelligent.

5. In this story the word **interchangeably** means
   - a. to mean different things.
   - b. to mean the same things.
   - c. to exchange.

Name _____ **Date** _____

Sylvester

Read the paragraph. Then answer the questions.

Sylvester is the smartest kid on the whole block. Take this morning, for example. It began when Mr. Wilkins couldn't start his car. Sylvester knew right away what was wrong. "You're out of gas, Mr. Wilkins," he said. And he was right. A few minutes later, Sylvester solved the mystery of the missing clothespins for Mrs. Johnson. Then he fixed Christopher Lee's broken wagon. After that, he figured out what was wrong with Mrs. Miller's vacuum cleaner. Of course, he got it working again in no time at all. After lunch, Sylvester watched a quiz show on TV. He gave each answer even before the <u>contestants</u> on the show could ring their buzzers. Nobody else on the block could have done any of those things. That Sylvester sure is smart!

1. What do you think the main idea of the story is? _____

_____

2. What was wrong with Mr. Wilkin's car? _____

_____

3. Whose wagon was broken? _____

4. Suppose Sylvester appeared on a TV quiz show. What do you think might happen?

_____

5. What are *contestants?* _____

_____

Name_____ Date _____

Friends in Nature

Read the story. Then circle the correct answer to each question.

Many people are needlessly afraid of spiders. Most spiders are harmless, helpful creatures. They spin soft, silky webs for homes, egg cocoons, and trapping food. When a spider completes a web for a trap, it covers the web with sticky silk. Then it waits for an insect to fly in and get caught. Once the insect is trapped, the spider ties it up with bands of silk, then gobbles it up.

The spider is really one of our best friends in nature. The insects it eats are harmful to us. Spiders eat grasshoppers and locusts which destroy our crops, and flies and mosquitoes which carry disease.

Not all spiders build webs to catch insects. Some, such as jumping spiders and wolf spiders, chase and catch their <u>prey</u> on the ground. Crab spiders hide in flowers to wait for butterflies or bees. Fisher spiders walk along the top of water and jump after insects and small fish.

1. Think about the story. What is it mostly about? Pick a good title.
    a. Jumping Spiders
    b. Spider Habits
    c. Afraid of Spiders

2. Spiders' webs
    a. are food traps.
    b. are not important to the spider.
    c. destroy our crops.

3. _____ catch their insects on the ground.
    a. Wolf spiders
    b. Crab spiders
    c. Fisher spiders

4. A spider would probably be helpful to have
    a. in a supermarket.
    b. in a garden.
    c. in school.

5. The word **prey** means
    a. mates.
    b. to plead.
    c. something hunted and caught for food

Name _____ **Date** _____

Nicky & the Musical Mice

Read the paragraph. Then answer the questions.

Every record made by Nicky and the Musical Mice has been a big hit. At least two of their songs are on the top ten list each week. Right now, no other rock group has as many records on the pop charts. Kids in every state belong to Mice fan clubs and wear Mice tee shirts. Every Mice concert is sold out an hour after the tickets go on sale. After each concert, thousands of cheering fans crowd around the Mice as they move from the stage door to their bus. All the Mice always take time out to sign hundreds of autographs before making their way through the noisy <u>throng</u>. Nicky and the Musical Mice is a very popular rock group.

1. Which sentence in the story sums up the main idea of the story?

_____

_____

2. How many songs by Nicky and the Musical Mice are on the top ten list each week?

_____

3. About how long does it take for all the tickets for a Musical Mice concert to be sold

out? _____

4. How do you think Nicky and the other members of the Musical Mice feel about their

fans? Why do you think so? _____

_____

5. What would be a good definition for the word *throng*? _____

_____

Name_____ Date _____

Starfish

Read the story. Then circle the correct answer to each question.

There are many kinds of starfish that live in the sea. A starfish body has a central disk and arms. Most starfish have five arms and look very much like stars. But some have as many as 50 arms and do not <u>resemble</u> stars at all.

Under each starfish arm are many thin tubes. At the end of these tubes are suction disks. The starfish uses these tube feet to crawl along the ocean floor. Starfish have a central opening or "mouth" on the undersides of their bodies. This mouth leads into a large stomach. Starfish eat shelled animals such as oysters, mussels, and clams. They use their tube feet to pull apart the shells, then push their stomachs into the shells to absorb the meat.

One of the most unusual things about the starfish is its ability to *regenerate* (grow again). If a starfish arm breaks off, the starfish will grow a new one in its place. If a starfish is cut in two, each of the pieces will grow into a new animal.

1. A good title for this story would be
   a. Let's Look at a Starfish
   b. Oysters, Mussels, and Clams
   c. New Habitats for the Starfish

2. Starfish live in
   a. rivers.
   b. oceans.
   c. lakes.

3. If a starfish loses an arm, it will
   a. die.
   b. be unable to eat.
   c. grow a new one.

4. Starfish probably present problems to
   a. people who raise oysters.
   b. scuba divers.
   c. astronomers.

5. **Resemble** means
   a. belong to the same family.
   b. gather together.
   c. look alike.

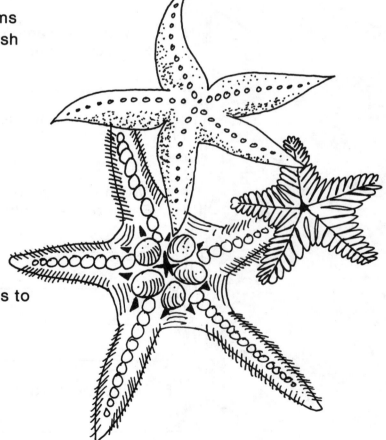

Name _____ Date _____

Let Your Hair Down

Read the paragraph. Then answer the questions.

Some people used to let their hair grow down to their knees. And some even let their hair grow so long that it reached down to their feet. But no one in history ever had hair that was longer than Rapunzel's. A wicked witch had locked Rapunzel in a tower. While she was <u>confined</u> there, Rapunzel let her hair grow longer and longer. Finally her hair reached all the way from the tower window down to the ground. She had so much hair that she used up two bottles of shampoo every morning when she washed her hair. It took all afternoon for her long hair to dry. And it took Rapunzel all evening just to comb through her hair. But she kept working at it until she was finished.

1. Underline the sentence that states the topic, or main thought, that is developed in this paragraph.

2. How much shampoo did Rapunzel use each time she washed her hair?

   _____

3. How long did it take Rapunzel's hair to dry.

   _____

4. Which of the following character traits do you think Rapunzel had: selfishness, honesty, patience, or curiosity?

   _____ Tell why you think so:

   _____

   _____

   _____

5. Define the word *confined.*

   _____

   _____

Name _____ Date _____

Talk to the Animals

Read the story. Then circle the correct answer to each question.

Can animals talk? They can't talk the way humans do. But they can communicate with each other—through sound, odor, and movement. Through the years, scientists have learned a lot about animal "talk." What is still a mystery is whether animals can be taught to "talk" with humans. Some people think they can.

No one expects animals to say words people can understand. Scientists are teaching them other ways to tell us what they need and want. Some chimps are being taught to punch words on a computer to send messages to humans. Gorillas are learning to use sign language.

Why do scientists want to talk with animals? Scientists still have a lot to learn about how the human brain works. Then they can help people who have difficulty learning to speak, read, and write. By solving the mysteries of animal languages, scientists hope to be able to solve some of the mysteries of our language.

1. An important idea of this story is:
    a. Some animals are learning to use computers.
    b. Some animals are learning to communicate with people.
    c. Scientists are learning little about the human brain.

2. Scientists have learned a great deal about
    a. the mysteries of our language.
    b. how animals communicate with humans.
    c. how animals communicate with animals.

3. Chimps are learning to send messages by
    a. using sign language.
    b. writing letters.
    c. using computers.

4. You can guess that gorillas and chimps are
    a. intelligent animals.
    b. lazy animals.
    c. good pets.

5. In this story, the word **punch** means
    a. to hit with your fist.
    b. to press keys.
    c. a tool for making holes.

Name_____ **Date** _____

Unfortunate Felix

Read the paragraph. Then answer the questions.

On Monday, the teacher scolded Felix for not doing his homework. On Tuesday, Felix threw food in the lunchroom, and he had to stay after school for that. On Wednesday, he was running in the halls, so he had to stay after school again. Then on Thursday, he fell asleep right in the middle of math class. He got his third <u>detention</u> of the week for that. On Friday, he cheated on a test. So he was sent to the principal's office. Felix always seems to be in some kind of trouble!

1. Circle the sentence that expresses the main idea best.

    a) Felix didn't do his homework on Monday.

    b) Someone caught Felix running in the halls.

    c) Felix is always in trouble.

2. Why did Felix have to stay after school on Tuesday? _____

_____

3. In which class did Felix fall asleep? _____

4. What kind of grades do you think Felix probably gets in most of his classes? Tell why

   you think so. _____

_____

_____

_____

5. In your own words, explain what a *detention* is. _____

_____

Name_____ **Date** _____

The Mysterious Monarchs

Read the story. Then circle the correct answer to each question.

In summer, thousands of people across the U.S. watch monarch butterflies float over gardens and fields. When summer ends, these bright orange and black butterflies disappear. Where do they go? Like many birds, they fly south in winter to escape the cold.

Every fall, millions of monarchs from all over the eastern U.S. and southern Canada leave their homes. They <u>migrate</u> south to Mexico. For some, the trip may take several months. They fly up to 3,000 miles altogether. They all meet on a mountainside north of Mexico City. They meet at the same place every year. Temperatures stay near freezing in this winter home. The monarchs hang on trees, resting. They save their energy to fly north again in spring.

It took scientists many years to discover where the monarchs go each winter. But one mystery still remains. Most scientists believe that as they fly back north, mother monarchs lay eggs. Then one by one, all the adult monarchs die. But the eggs hatch and the new monarchs continue the trip north. If this is true, how do the new butterflies know where to go for the summer? And how are they able to find the wooded hillside north of Mexico City in the fall?

1. A good title for this story is
   a. How to Catch Butterflies.
   b. How the Monarch Mystery was Solved
   c. The Monarchs' Winter Home

2. Monarch butterflies are
   a. fast fliers.
   b. orange and black.
   c. black and white.

3. The monarchs' winter home is in
   a. Mexico.
   b. Canada.
   c. eastern U.S.

4. You can guess that scientists are
   a. studying the weather in Mexico City.
   b. no longer studying the monarch butterfly.
   c. still studying the monarch butterfly.

5. The best definition for the word **migrate** is
   a. move.
   b. look.
   c. grind.

Name_____ Date _____

11

A Circus Dream

Read the paragraph. Then answer the questions.

For as long as she can remember, Betsy has always wanted to be in the circus. When she was nine, she dreamed of being a clown with a big red nose and a polka-dot suit. "Everybody loves a clown," she said. When she was ten, she wanted to be a lion trainer. "I would even be brave enough to put my head right in the lion's mouth!" she boasted. At eleven, she wanted to dance with the elephants. "I'll sit on the biggest pachyderm's head as it dances around the ring," she declared. At twelve, she wanted to be in either the flying trapeze act or the high wire act. Today, at eighty-five years of age, Betsy still dreams of joining the circus.

1. Which sentence tells the main idea of the paragraph?

_____

2. What details are given to describe the clown Betsy dreamed of being? _____

_____

3. How old was Betsy when she wanted to be a lion trainer? _____

4. Did Betsy ever join the circus? Explain your answer.

_____

_____

_____

5. The word *pachyderm* is used in the paragraph. Can you figure out what it means?

Write another word for *pachyderm* on this line: _____

_____

_____

Name_____ **Date** _____

Unusual Animals

Read the story. Then circle the correct answer to each question.

Some of the truly <u>unique</u> animals in the world live in Australia. Most of them are marsupials, or "pouched mammals." A female marsupial has a pouch on her abdomen. She feeds and cares for her young in this pouch. Kangaroos are the most well-known marsupials. The koala, which is often mistakenly thought to be a bear, is a marsupial, too.

One of the unusual Australian animals is the platypus. It has a beak like a duck and webbed feet like an otter. It has a tail like a bear. It lays eggs, unlike most mammals. There is only one other egg-laying mammal alive today: the echidna, or spiny anteater. It, too, lives in Australia.

Long ago, a bridge of land connected Australia with mainland Asia. But that bridge disappeared before most of today's mammals appeared. That's why the animals on this island continent are so unique.

1. A good title for this story could be
   - a. Hopping Kangaroos
   - b. Some Animals of Australia
   - c. The Island Continent

2. Most of Australia's native animals
   - a. lay eggs.
   - b. are bears.
   - c. are marsupials.

3. Koalas are related to
   - a. bears.
   - b. reptiles.
   - c. kangaroos.

4. You can guess that most mammals
   - a. do not lay eggs.
   - b. have pouches.
   - c. live in Australia.

5. The best definition for the word
   unique is
   - a. one of a kind.
   - b. similar.
   - c. bring together.

Name_____ **Date** _____

The Country Fair

Read the paragraph. Then answer the questions.

At the fair, Marcus saw horses, cows, sheep, and goats. He saw ducks, geese, chickens, and turkeys—and then he saw dogs. Of all the animals he saw at the fair, Marcus liked the dogs best. He liked the way the dogs barked when he came into view—the horse and cows didn't do that. He liked the way the dogs wagged their tails when he came near—the sheep and goats didn't do that. He liked the way the dogs licked his face when he stopped to say hello—the ducks and geese didn't do that. And he liked the way each dog sat still while he patted its head and rubbed its ears and <u>chucked</u> it under its chin. The chickens and turkeys didn't do that.

1. A topic sentence is a sentence that states the principal topic or main idea of a paragraph. Underline the topic sentence in the paragraph above.

2. Where did Horace see all these animals? _____

3. List three things that Horace liked about the dogs.

   _____

   _____

   _____

4. Suppose Horace was walking home from school and he saw someone teasing a stray dog. What do you think he would do? Explain why you think he would do it.

   _____

   _____

   _____

5. What do you think the word *chucked* means as it is used in this paragraph? _____

   _____

Name_____ **Date** _____

A Bear From China

Read the story. Then circle the correct answer to each question.

The giant panda is a large, black and white, woolly animal that looks like a cuddly teddy bear. Most giant pandas live high in the evergreen forests of western China. They live mostly on the ground and feed on some plants and animals. But their main food is bamboo, which grows in the damp, cool, moist forest. The giant panda has an "extra" thumb—a sixth <u>digit</u> on each of its front feet that lets it grab and hold bamboo shoots.

The Chinese call the giant panda a *bei-shung*. This means *white bear.* Giant pandas are shaped like bears, and they move in the same slow, clumsy way. Also like bears, they can stand on their two hind feet. But scientists are not sure whether the giant panda is really a bear, or more closely related to the raccoon. Its teeth and some other features are much like those of a raccoon.

No one knows for sure how many giant pandas there are in the wild, but they are thought to be rare. In 1972 China gave a gift to the people of the United States: two giant pandas.

1. A good title for this story would be
    a. An Extra Thumb
    b. The Giant Panda
    c. Ling-Ling and Hsing-Hsing

2. Most giant pandas live
    a. in zoos.
    b. in trees.
    c. on the ground.

3. *Bei-shung* means
    a. giant bear.
    b. white bear.
    c. extra thumb.

4. Scientists probably want to
    a. learn more about the
       giant panda.
    b. put all pandas in zoos.
    c. learn more about raccoons.

5. In this story the word **digit** means
    a. a number symbol.
    b. a finger or toe.
    c. to understand.

Name_____ Date _____

Julie Goes Shopping

Read the paragraph. Then answer the questions.

Halloween was coming. All of Julie's friends had already bought their pumpkins. Julie wanted to find a pumpkin that was bigger than anyone else's. First, she looked in the supermarket. There were only three pumpkins left, and they were all very small. "What <u>diminutive</u> pumpkins!" said Julie. Then she went to Mr. Clark's Fruit Stand. The biggest pumpkin Mr. Clark had wasn't big enough, so Julie said, "I want a bigger pumpkin than that." Next, she walked into Marco's Friendly Grocery Store. A moment later, she came out with a sad look on her face. Finally, she decided to go out to Peterson's Pumpkin Farm. "I will walk up and down the rows of pumpkins in the pumpkin patch until I find the biggest pumpkin of all," she said.

1. Which of the following three titles tells what the story is mostly about? Draw a circle around it.

    a) Julie's Friends

    b) Mr. Clark's Fruit Stand

    c) The Biggest Pumpkin

2. How many pumpkins were left in the supermarket when Julie looked there? _____

3. What was the last place Julie decided to look for a pumpkin.

_____

4. Why do you think Julie looked sad when she came out of Marco's Friendly Grocery Store?

_____

_____

5. Julie said the pumpkins in the supermarket were *diminutive*. What did she mean?

_____

Name_____ **Date** _____

Animal Camouflage

Read the story. Then circle the correct answer to each question.

How do animals keep safe? One way is through camouflage. The color or shape of some animals' bodies makes them look like part of their <u>natural</u> homes. This hides them from their enemies. A fawn's white spots, for example, blend with the sunlight in the forest. This breaks up the outline of the fawn's body, making it hard to see. Certain insects, such as moths and katydids, are the same color as the leaves they feed on. Other insects are shaped like their surroundings. An insect called a tree-hopper looks very much like a thorn on a branch. A walking stick looks like a twig.

Some animals can change the color of their bodies to blend with their surroundings. This is especially helpful to an animal whose surroundings change from season to season. The snowshoe hare is one such animal. In summer the hare's fur is brown. It matches the rocks of the woods in which it lives. In fall the rabbit's fur gets lighter. By winter it is white to match the snow.

1. A good title for this story could be
    a. The Snowshoe Hare
    b. Hidden Animals
    c. Insect Shapes

2. If an animal can blend in with its surroundings
    a. it may not be able to find food.
    b. it will be easy to see.
    c. it may keep safe from its enemies.

3. An animal whose shape camouflages it is the
    a. snowshoe hare.
    b. fawn.
    c. walking stick.

4. You can guess that the snowshoe hare
    a. lives where it is warm all year.
    b. lives where it snows in winter.
    c. lives in trees.

5. In this story the word **natural** means
    a. simple.
    b. in nature.
    c. the whole country.

Name_____ **Date** _____

A Mountain Meadow

Read the paragraph. Then answer the questions.

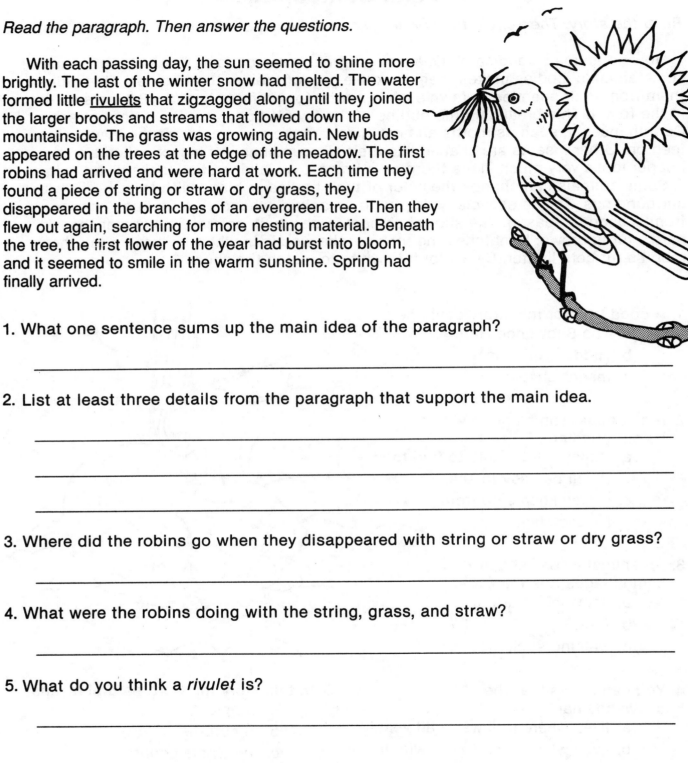

With each passing day, the sun seemed to shine more brightly. The last of the winter snow had melted. The water formed little <u>rivulets</u> that zigzagged along until they joined the larger brooks and streams that flowed down the mountainside. The grass was growing again. New buds appeared on the trees at the edge of the meadow. The first robins had arrived and were hard at work. Each time they found a piece of string or straw or dry grass, they disappeared in the branches of an evergreen tree. Then they flew out again, searching for more nesting material. Beneath the tree, the first flower of the year had burst into bloom, and it seemed to smile in the warm sunshine. Spring had finally arrived.

1. What one sentence sums up the main idea of the paragraph?

_____

2. List at least three details from the paragraph that support the main idea.

_____

_____

_____

3. Where did the robins go when they disappeared with string or straw or dry grass?

_____

4. What were the robins doing with the string, grass, and straw?

_____

5. What do you think a *rivulet* is?

_____

Name_____ **Date** _____

The Largest Seal

Read the story. Then circle the correct answer to each question.

The largest member of the seal family is the elephant seal. The southern elephant seal lives in the icy waters of Antarctica. It is the larger of two species. The northern elephant seal lives in the Pacific Ocean along the coast of California. The male may grow to be 15 feet (4.6 m) long and weigh up to 6,000 pounds (2700 kg).

Like all seals, the elephant seal is a warm-blooded mammal. It breathes air. It lives in water and on land. In the water, the animal's front flippers help it swim. On land, the elephant seal uses them like hands. It uses its flippers to scratch its nose or clean its fur, to scoop up sand to throw at an annoying insect, and to cover its body with sand while lying on the beach. The hind flippers help the elephant seal to move from place to place. In the ocean these flippers help the animal dive deep to the ocean bottom to find food—squid, dogfish, skates, and ratfish.

The elephant seal is named for its long, curved nose. This "trunk" helps the animals make a strange, loud noise. Its course, <u>tough</u> skin may also look like elephant hide.

1. A good title for this story is
    a. All About Flippers
    b. Animal Trunks
    c. Elephant Seals

2. The elephant seal is a
    a. kind of elephant.
    b. kind of seal.
    c. kind of fish.

3. The northern elephant seal lives
    a. in the icy north.
    b. in Antarctica.
    c. along the California coast.

4. A 20-foot long elephant seal is probably
    a. too big to swim.
    b. a northern elephant seal.
    c. a southern elephant seal.

5. In this story the word **tough** means
    a. too bad.
    b. hard.
    c. bold.

Name_____ **Date** _____

Twinkle Toes

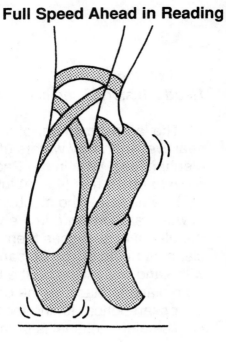

Read the paragraph. Then answer the questions.

Irene loved to dance, and everyone agreed she was a pretty good dancer. But Fran could dance better. Flo had taken dancing lessons for six years, and she was the best dancer on her block. But Fran could dance better than Flo. Mrs. Snootful insisted no one could dance better than her daughter, Myrna. But Fran could do it. In fact, Fran could dance better than anyone in the entire state. She had even won a trophy that proved she could. She had won it in a state-wide dance <u>competition</u> against some talented contestants. Each of the dancers had graduated at the top of his or her class in dancing school.

1. In your own words, state the main idea of the paragraph.

   _____

2. What was Mrs. Snootful's daughter's first name? _____

3. What detail supports the idea that Fran had been up against some "talented" contestants. _____

   _____

4. Based on the facts contained in the paragraph, would you say that Fran lived on the same block as Flo? Explain your answer. _____

   _____

   _____

5. Give a definition for the word *competition* as it is used in the paragraph above.

   _____

   _____

   _____

Name_____ **Date** _____

Sweet Treats

Read the story. Then circle the correct answer to each question.

Ice cream is America's favorite dessert. It is said that during his travels through China in the 13th century, Marco Polo tasted ices made from water and milk. He brought recipes for these ices back to Italy with him. They spread through Europe. Soon cream and butter were added, and the dish was called cream ice.

In the early 1700's, ice cream became a popular treat in America. The ice-cream soda may have been born in 1874. At that time, a man in Philadelphia mixed soda water and ice cream. In some places this treat could not be sold on Sundays. So a clever shopkeeper in Illinois left out the soda water and served ice cream with syrup. He called his dish a "Sunday," later to become a "sundae." It is thought that the ice-cream cone was invented at a fair in St. Louis, Missouri, in 1904. An ice-cream seller at the fair ran out of plates on which to serve the ice cream. His <u>stand</u> happened to be next to the waffle stand. So he rolled waffles and filled them with ice cream.

No one knows for sure who invented ice cream. We're just glad it was invented!

1. A good title for this story is
   - a. Ice Cream Flavors
   - b. The History of Ice Cream
   - c. Ice Cream and Waffles

2. In the early 1700's, ice cream became popular in
   - a. China.
   - b. Europe.
   - c. America.

3. The ice-cream cone may have been invented in
   - a. Philadelphia.
   - b. Italy.
   - c. St. Louis.

4. You can guess that people
   - a. in Philadelphia liked soda water.
   - b. liked ice-cream sodas but not ice-cream cones.
   - c. liked the new ways to serve ice cream.

5. In this story the word **stand** means
   - a. the opposite of sit.
   - b. a booth.
   - c. to rank.

Name_____ **Date** _____

The Mysterious Neighbor

Read the paragraph. Then answer the questions.

No one had ever seen Sally Simoleon. She lived all alone in a huge mansion, surrounded by beautiful gardens and wide lawns. A high wall went all the way around her property, and there was a huge iron gate at the entrance. No one could get in unless the guard opened the gate. And he had orders not to open it for anyone except the servants. Sally had dozens of servants, but none of them had ever caught a glimpse of her. Even Jeeves, the servant who brought her meals to her, never saw her. He set her food out on the dining room table and then <u>withdrew</u> before she came down to dinner. The neighbors all wondered what Sally looked like, too. But she never invited them to visit her, and she did not accept when they invited her to visit them.

1. Which sentence states the main idea of the paragraph—the first or the last sentence?

   _____

2. What kept people off Ms. Simoleon's property? _____

   _____

3. What was the butler's name? _____

4. Which of the following conclusions can you draw, based on the facts presented in the paragraph? Circle your choice.

   a) Ms. Simoleon was a ghost.

   b) Ms. Simoleon was very ugly.

   c) Ms. Simoleon was very rich.

5. What other word could have been used instead of the word *withdrew* to describe what

   the butler did after he set Ms. Simoleon's food on the table? _____

   _____

Name_____ **Date** _____

What Are Dreams?

Read the story. Then circle the correct answer to each question.

Everyone dreams. Some dreams are scary and some are annoying. Others are funny. Still other dreams don't seem to make any sense at all. You probably don't remember all your dreams—but you have them every night! During eight hours of sleep, you may have as many as five dreams.

Your dreams are like stories made up of your own experiences and feelings. Although you <u>participate</u> in some dreams, you just "watch" what happens in others. In most dreams you feel that you have no control over what happens.

Scientists can't see your dreams, but they are able to tell when you are dreaming. Some scientists think that dreams are stories we tell ourselves. They may be about something that happened to us the day before the dream. They may be about things we wish for. Or they may be about our fears. Other scientists say that dreams don't mean much at all. No one knows for sure what dreams mean. But scientists keep working to learn what our "sleep stories" are all about.

1. A good title for this story is
   a. Funny Dreams
   b. Sleep Stories
   c. Nightmares

2. In one night you may have
   a. no dreams.
   b. more than eight dreams.
   c. up to five dreams.

3. Scientists are able to tell
   a. why you dream.
   b. when you dream.
   c. what you dream.

4. You can guess that your dreams
   a. are not like anyone else's dreams.
   b. are always the same.
   c. always make sense.

5. The best definition for the word **participate** is
   a. share.
   b. take part in.
   c. celebrate.

Name_____ Date _____

Good Grief, Gus!

Read the paragraph. Then answer the questions.

Gus has a big appetite. Every morning he eats two dozen eggs. Then he eats a big slab of bacon. A pile of hash brown potatoes comes next. He also eats a dozen slices of toast with jelly. Along with this "small" breakfast, he drinks a glass of juice and three glasses of milk. For lunch, he <u>consumes</u> four or five sandwiches. Each one is loaded with cold cuts, mayonnaise, lettuce, tomatoes, and cheese. He has a dozen donuts and two milk shakes for an afternoon snack. His dinner is ten pork chops or twelve hamburgers or fifteen hot dogs smothered in sauerkraut. He also eats a mountain of mashed potatoes and a big bowl of green or yellow vegetables. For dessert he has a whole box of cookies and a container of ice cream.

1. The topic sentence states the main topic or most important idea discussed in a paragraph. Underline the topic sentence in the paragraph above.

2. What kinds of meat does Gus eat at dinner? _____

_____

_____

3. What does Gus have for dessert? _____

_____

4. Gus's friend, Pat, went on a diet. Pat ate a grapefruit for breakfast, and yogurt for lunch. Dinner was a small piece of fish, a baked potato, and half a cup of green beans. If Gus had to go on the same diet, how do you think he would feel? Why?

_____

_____

_____

5. Synonyms are words that have the same or nearly the same meanings. What is a

synonym for the word *consumes?* _____

Name_____ **Date** _____

A Folk Hero

Read the story. Then circle the correct answer to each question.

John Chapman was born in Massachusetts in 1774. His father was a farmer. John enjoyed helping around the farm. He especially liked to help in the apple orchard. John Chapman loved apple trees!

When John was a young man, pioneer wagons passed his farm. They were on their way to the Ohio Valley. John gave the settlers apple seeds and hoped they would plant them. But with all the other things they had to do, it didn't seem likely the settlers would have much time for planting apple trees.

One day it <u>occurred</u> to John that he could go to the Ohio Valley himself and plant apple orchards. John collected seeds from cider mills. He dried them and put them into small bags. He walked hundreds of miles to the Ohio Valley. He made many friends along the way. He gave bags of apple seeds to everyone he met. John planted many apple seeds himself. Soon he became known by his frontier neighbors as Johnny Appleseed.

1. A good title for this story is
   a. How to Grow Apple Trees
   b. The Story of Johnny Appleseed
   c. Wagon Train

2. Johnny Appleseed was born in
   a. Ohio.
   b. Pennsylvania.
   c. Massachusetts.

3. Johnny Appleseed traveled by
   a. car.
   b. wagon train.
   c. foot.

4. John Chapman was called Johnny Appleseed because
   a. the pioneers couldn't pronounce "Chapman."
   b. he chopped down apple trees.
   c. he loved growing apple trees.

5. In this story the word **occurred** means
   a. forgot.
   b. came to mind.
   c. announced.

Name_____ **Date** _____

A Strange Thing

Read the paragraph. Then answer the questions.

Sometimes Lana has a box of gumdrops in her hand or a bag of hard candies in her pocket. Sometimes she has marshmallows or candy corn or jellybeans. Once, I saw her with a bag of those little bite-sized chocolate bars. Another time, she was holding a big can of peanut brittle. I don't think I ever saw her without some kind of sweet snack. I never know what kind of <u>confection</u> she'll have next—either in her hands or stuffed in her pocket or sticking out of her purse. The strange thing is that Lana hates sweets! She never eats them. She just carries them around in case she meets someone who has a sweet tooth!

1. Make up a new title for the paragraph. Try to think of one that gives a good idea of what the paragraph is about.

   _____

2. Several kinds of sweets are named in the paragraph. Can you list three of them?

   _____

   _____

   _____

3. What was in the can that Lana was holding? _____

4. Based on the information provided in the paragraph, which of the following conclusions might you draw? Circle your choice and then explain your answer.

   a) Lana is selfish.   _____

   b) Lana is smart.   _____

   c) Lana is cheap.   _____

   d) Lana is thoughtful. _____

5. By the way the word *confection* is used in the paragraph, can you decide what it means? Write a good definition below.

   _____

Name_____   Date _____

Fight or Flight

Read the story. Then circle the correct answer to each question.

It's your turn to give a speech in front of the assembly today. Suddenly your mouth goes dry as you are walking to school. You feel as though there are butterflies in your stomach. You step off the curb to cross the street, and a speeding bicycle nearly hits you. Your heart begins to pound. What are these feelings and why do you get them?

When you become nervous, frightened, or upset, your body gets ready. It prepares to think fast, fight back, or run away. It sends a special chemical messenger (a hormone called adrenalin) into your blood stream. The message says: "Emergency! My heart, lungs, and muscles need more strength. Send food!" And your body starts to pump extra blood to these organs. The blood contains oxygen and sugar to give you more strength and energy. Your heart beats faster. At the same time, body functions that are less <u>vital</u> slow down for a while. Your body stops producing saliva, so your mouth becomes dry. Your digestion stops, too. This leaves you with a strange feeling in your stomach.

1. A good title for this story could be
   a. Understanding Hormones
   b. Monarch Butterflies
   c. How Your Body Prepares
      for Emergencies

2. Adrenalin is a kind of hormone that
   a. helps digest food.
   b. acts as a messenger.
   c. produces saliva.

3. You get a strange feeling in your stomach when you're nervous because
   a. your digestion stops.
   b. your digestion speeds up.
   c. you stop producing saliva.

4. Which of the situations below would most likely send adrenalin into your blood stream?
   a. You are waiting for the dentist to drill your teeth.
   b. You are waiting for your favorite TV show to begin.
   c. You are listening to records.

5. In this story the word **vital** means
   a. necessary.
   b. energetic.
   c. colorful.

Name_____ Date _____

27

Jeffrey's Surprise

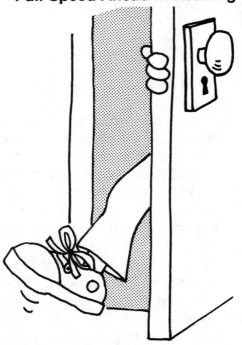

Read the paragraph. Then answer the questions.

When Jeffrey was in the fifth grade, he wasn't very popular. For some unknown reason, he was unfriendly, <u>impolite,</u> and selfish. Over the summer, however, Jeffrey really changed. When he walked into Mr. Green's sixth grade class on the first day of school, he was a different person. He had become both friendly *and* polite. Best of all, he had become a person who really seemed to care about people.

1. Which of the following sentences best expresses the main idea of the paragraph? Circle your choice.

    a.   Jeffrey wasn't very popular.

    b.   Jeffrey changed a lot over the summer vacation.

    c.   Jeffrey was unfriendly and selfish.

2. What details describe the kind of personality Jeffrey had when he was in the fifth grade? _____

_____

3. What was the name of the sixth-grade teacher? _____

4. Based on the information in the paragraph, how do you think Jeffrey will get along with the other members of his sixth-grade class? _____

_____

5. What does the word *impolite* mean? _____

_____

Name_____ Date _____

Strange Plants

Read the story. Then circle the correct answer to each question.

Some plants—called carnivorous (meat-eating) plants—trap insects for food. Like most green plants, meat-eating plants need air, water, and sunshine to grow. They also need certain minerals, especially nitrogen. Most plants get the nitrogen they need from the soil. But most carnivorous plants grow in warm, moist places where the soil has <u>insufficient</u> nitrogen. These plants must get nitrogen in other ways.

Meat-eating plants give off sweet odors. These smells attract insects. Once an insect lands on a carnivorous plant, it is in trouble! The Venus's-flytrap, for example, has leaves that close tightly around the insect, trapping it inside. The sundew plant has sticky hairs which catch the insect. Then the leaves start to curl around the insect, trapping it inside. The tube-shaped leaves of the pitcher plant collect water in which the insect drowns.

Carnivorous plants give off digestive juices which suffocate the insect and then dissolve its body. The nitrogen and other minerals from the insect's body are then absorbed by the plant.

1. Think about the story. What is it mostly about? Pick a good title.
    - a. Nitrogen Capers
    - b. Pretty Plants
    - c. Plants That Eat Insects

2. Most plants get nitrogen from
    - a. the air.
    - b. the soil.
    - c. animal tissue.

3. Carnivorous plants give off digestive juices which help
    - a. trap the insects.
    - b. attract the insects.
    - c. dissolve the insects' bodies.

4. Carnivorous plants probably do not grow in
    - a. jungles.
    - b. swamps.
    - c. deserts.

5. The word **insufficient** means
    - a. not enough.
    - b. adequate.
    - c. too much.

Name_____ **Date** _____

A Big Secret

Read the paragraph. Then answer the questions.

Jake was the manager at the Soyburger Snack Shop. But he didn't know the secret formula for the famous soyburger super sauce. Hank cooked the burgers on the <u>griddle</u> in the Snack Shop. But he didn't know the formula for the sauce. Tess took customers' orders for soyburgers and other snacks. But she didn't know the secret super sauce formula. Terri squirted the super sauce on top of every burger sold at the Snack Shop. But she didn't know how to make it. Roger wrapped the burgers. Sally served them. Wanda wiped the tables. But Roger, Sally, and Wanda didn't know the secret formula for the sauce. No one knew the secret formula except the man who invented it—Sheldon Soyburger.

1. In your own words, write a sentence that tells the main idea of the paragraph. _____

_____

2. Who took the customers' orders for snacks? _____

3. What was Terri's job at the Soyburger Snack Shop? _____

_____

4. Based on the information in the paragraph, why do you think the place is named the

Soyburger Snack Shop? _____

_____

5. Judging by the way the word *griddle* is used in the paragraph, give a brief explanation of a *griddle* here?

_____

_____

Name_____ **Date** _____

Stones of Mystery

Read the story. Then circle the correct answer to each question.

If you visit southern England you will probably see Stonehenge. It is a circle of huge, cut stones that was <u>erected</u> more than 3,500 years ago.

Scientists do not know for sure how Stonehenge was built or why it was built. They do know that it took a great deal of skill and technical knowledge to build it. The huge rocks that form the circle weigh many tons. They were brought to Stonehenge from many miles away. Scientists can guess that they were carried on large log platforms, each pulled by ropes held by hundreds of people. Small stones were probably used to shape the giant ones.

Some scientists think the monument was used as a kind of calendar. The calendar may have let ancient people predict seasons of the year and eclipses of the sun and moon. Whatever it was used for, Stonehenge is one of the most amazing structures that people have ever made!

1. A good title for this story is
   - a. Sightseeing in England
   - b. Using a Calendar
   - c. Amazing Stonehenge

2. Many scientists think Stonehenge was used
   - a. as a palace.
   - b. as a calendar.
   - c. to keep out enemies.

3. Stonehenge is located in
   - a. southern Europe.
   - b. southern England.
   - c. northern England.

4. Small stones were probably used to cut the giant rocks because
   - a. that's the best way to cut rocks.
   - b. the builders had no metal tools.
   - c. the builders had many extra small stones.

5. In this story the word **erected** means
   - a. built.
   - b. discovered.
   - c. used.

Name_____ **Date** _____

A Sweet Tale

Read the paragraph. Then answer the questions.

Louise stood in front of the candy counter, looking at all the candies. There were dozens of kinds, all neatly arranged in a big glass case. "I'll get some gumdrops," she thought. "No, I think I'll get some of those delicious licorice sticks instead." But when she saw some very expensive chocolate-covered cherries, she <u>queried</u>, "Should I get some of those?" Even before she could answer her own question, her eyes happened to land on the peanut-butter cups. "I'll get some of those instead," she thought. But then she changed her mind again. "I'll get some jellybeans," she thought, "or maybe a few bonbons." Her eyes darted from one kind of candy to another. "Oh dear," she said.

1. Circle the sentence that best expresses the main idea of the paragraph.

    a) Louise liked the way the candies were arranged.

    b) Louise thought the licorice sticks looked delicious.

    c) Louise couldn't decide what kind of candy to buy.

2. Where were the candies neatly arranged? _____

3. Louise saw some very expensive candies. What kind were they?

    _____

4. One day someone passed a box of chocolates to Louise and said, "Would you like to try one?" There were ten different kinds of chocolates in the box. What do you think happened?

    _____

    _____

5. Find the word *queried* in the paragraph and decide what it means. Write your

    definition here: _____

Name_____ **Date** _____

Rough Riders

Read the story. Then circle the correct answer to each question.

Watch out—here they come! They are racing through mud, around curves, down hills, and over bumps. These boys and girls are riding bicycle motocross—BMX for short. BMX-ers ride special bikes on dirt tracks. The bikes are smaller, stronger, and lighter weight than regular bikes. The tires are thick and <u>knobby</u> for rough riding in the dirt.

For safety, BMX-ers wear special clothes. They wear helmets, long-sleeved shirts, and mouth protectors. Most racers wear gloves, knee pads, and elbow pads, too. Some racers wear goggles.

Unlike baseball and hockey—which are team sports—BMX is an individual sport. Racers compete in groups based on their age, experience, and ability. Special bicycle clubs run local and national races. They make rules about the tracks, bikes, and safety equipment. The rules make sure that races are fair and safe. Racers compete to collect points. The ones with the most points may win plaques, trophies, or ribbons.

1. The main idea of the second paragraph is that
   a. goggles are not very important.
   b. most racers wear gloves and helmets.
   c. BMX-ers wear special clothing for safety.

2. A BMX track is
   a. one mile long.
   b. not flat and straight.
   c. indoors.

3. BMX bikes are
   a. heavier than regular bikes.
   b. lighter than regular bikes.
   c. bigger than regular bikes.

4. You can guess that a racer who is dressed properly
   a. will win the race.
   b. will look great.
   c. won't be badly hurt if he or she falls.

5. A definition for the word **knobby** is
   a. bumpy.
   b. like a door.
   c. smooth.

Name_____ **Date** _____

Vacation Blues

Read the paragraph. Then answer the questions.

A storm was coming. The first hint had been a slight change in the direction of the breeze. It had been a warm, southerly breeze, but it had swung around, and now it was coming from the west. It was cooler, too. The ocean was not as calm now as it had been a few minutes earlier. Whitecaps began to appear on its surface, and the waves seemed to pound the shore more angrily than usual. Sudden gusts of wind <u>buffeted</u> the people on the beach, nearly knocking them over. Dark clouds rolled across the sky, blocking out the sun's warm rays. Jonathan quickly stood up and began to gather his things together.

1. Which of the following sentences states the main idea? Circle your choice.

    a) A storm was coming.

    b) The ocean was not as calm now as it had been a few minutes earlier.

    c) Jonathan quickly stood up and began to gather his things together.

2. List at least three details that support the main idea of the paragraph. _____

    _____

    _____

3. From what direction was the breeze coming after it had swung around? _____

4. Based on the information in the paragraph, what prediction can you make about what

    Jonathan will do next, and why? _____

    _____

    _____

5. Find the word *buffeted* in the paragraph. Judging by the way it is used, give a brief

    definition for the word here. _____

    _____

Name_____ **Date** _____

Let's Ride

Read the story. Then circle the correct answer to each question.

Rodeo is a Spanish word for "roundup." Rodeos are more than 100 years old.
They started in the West as a celebration when the work of roundup was done.
At first there were no set rules for rodeo. After a while some of the cowboys
began to choose rodeo as a profession. Rules were made. Clubs were formed to
make sure the rules were followed. Today rodeo cowboys and cowgirls compete
for big prize money. Belt buckles are given as prizes, too.

To win, rodeo contestants <u>match</u> their riding and roping skills in two main groups
of events. In *rough stock events* they try to ride bucking horses or bulls for
a certain length of time. They are awarded points for the way they ride.
Timed events are judged by how fast the contestant completes certain tasks,
such as roping a calf or a steer.

Rodeos are held in many parts of the United States and in Canada. Similar
contests are held in Australia. Junior rodeos, in which children compete, are held
mostly in the southwestern United States.

1. Think about the story. What is it
   mostly about? Pick a good title.
   - a. Junior Rodeos
   - b. Rodeo Events
   - c. Roping Skills

2. The word "rodeo" means
   - a. contest.
   - b. highway.
   - c. roundup.

3. In rough stock events riders
   - a. ride bucking horses.
   - b. rope calves.
   - c. rope steer.

4. You can guess that rodeo cowboys
   and cowgirls
   - a. know a lot about the old west.
   - b. must be tall.
   - c. know a lot about horses
     and cattle.

5. In this story the word **match** means
   - a. a strip of wood.
   - b. compete with.
   - c. a pair of like things.

Name_____ **Date** _____

Write It Right!

Read the paragraph. Then answer the questions.

When Fred made a mistake, he crossed it out and wrote something else in its place. Fran used an eraser and rubbed out any mistakes she made. When Flo made a mistake, she just crumpled up her paper and tossed it on the floor. But Fritz never made mistakes. Before he started writing, he thought about what he was going to write about. Then he wrote it, slowly and neatly. If he was unsure of the meaning or spelling of a word, he looked it up in a <u>lexicon</u> before he wrote it on his paper. He always made sure his subjects and verbs were in agreement, and he never used "I" or "me" incorrectly. He checked his facts before he wrote them down, and he double-checked any numbers to make sure they were right. When he was finished, he always proofread his paper before he handed it in.

1. Underline the one sentence that states the main idea of the paragraph.

2. What did Fritz do before he started writing? _____

_____

3. What did Fritz do when he was finished writing? _____

_____

_____

4. Based on the information in the paragraph, what kinds of grades do you think Fritz

normally receives? _____

_____

5. Write another word that means the same as *lexicon.* _____

_____

Name_____ **Date** _____

Dribble & Shoot

Read the story. Then circle the correct answer to each question.

Basketball is one of the most popular sports in the world. Did you ever wonder how the game got started? It was invented by James A. Naismith in 1891. Mr. Naismith was a gym teacher at a school in Springfield, Massachusetts. It was winter, and his students were not getting much exercise. So he thought of some rules for a team game that could be played indoors. He nailed two old peach baskets to the ends of the gym balcony. One basket belonged to each team. The idea of the game was for each team to <u>score</u> points by throwing the ball into their basket. At the same time, each team had to try to stop the other team from scoring.

The new game quickly became popular. When it was first played, each time a player scored someone had to climb a ladder to get the ball out of the basket. Soon wire mesh baskets replaced the peach baskets. After a while a net attached to a metal hoop was used. Many other changes have been made over the years. But the idea of basketball is still the same.

1. A good title for this story could be
    a. The Basketball Hall of Fame
    b. How Basketball Began
    c. The Story of James A. Naismith

2. In the earliest days of basketball
    a. wire mesh baskets were used as goals.
    b. metal hoops were used as goals.
    c. peach baskets were used as goals.

3. James A. Naismith was a
    a. math teacher.
    b. English teacher.
    c. gym teacher.

4. You can guess that using peach baskets made the game
    a. go slower.
    b. go faster.
    c. more exciting.

5. In this story the word **score** means
    a. to reject.
    b. to earn.
    c. a group of 20 items.

Name_____ **Date** _____

Summer Fun

Read the paragraph. Then answer the questions.

Maria's ice-cold lemonade was delicious. In fact, it was the best lemonade in town. She mixed it herself in the kitchen. It was made from these <u>ingredients:</u> freshly-squeezed lemons, sugar, water, and lots of ice. Maria brought one pitcher at a time out to her lemonade stand in the front yard. At 50¢ a glass, Maria's ice-cold lemonade sold as fast as she could make it. People even waited in long lines to buy it. After standing for a half hour in the hot sun, they would have been willing to pay almost anything for a glass of Maria's ice-cold lemonade.

1. Make up a new title. Try to think of one that helps express the main idea of the paragraph.

   _____

2. Where was Maria's lemonade stand located? _____

3. How much money did Maria charge for each glass of lemonade? _____

4. Based on the information in the paragraph, why would the people who waited in line be willing to pay almost anything for a glass of Maria's ice-cold lemonade?

   _____

   _____

5. Write a definition of the word *ingredients*. Can you think of one word that could be used in place of the word ingredients in the paragraph?_____

   _____

   _____

Name_____ **Date** _____

The New Athletes

Read the story. Then circle the correct answer to each question.

At one time, most sports were <u>reserved</u> for athletic people. But today, handicapped children and adults take part in the same sports as their friends. In sports such as basketball, tennis, and track and field, the "new" athletes may use braces, crutches, or wheelchairs. These help them move from place to place. In other sports, such as swimming and horseback riding, they can move freely.

People take part in sports for exercise, good mental health, and to have fun. Sports bring the same rewards to handicapped people. As a bonus, they get the satisfaction of doing something they never thought they could do.

Today, handicapped people take part in every sport you can think of. They compete with each other. They also compete in regular athletic events against other athletes. The most important thing in sports for the handicapped isn't winning. The main goal is to participate and to have fun!

1. A good title for this story is
   a. Sports for the Athlete
   b. Sports for the Handicapped
   c. Winning is Everything

2. Handicapped people can move more freely in sports such as
   a. basketball and tennis.
   b. swimming and horseback riding.
   c. track and field.

3. Today handicapped people can take part in
   a. all sports.
   b. some sports.
   c. no sports.

4. You can guess that the rules of most wheelchair games are
   a. a little different from the original game.
   b. the same as the original game.
   c. entirely different from the original game.

5. In this story the word *reserved* means
   a. set aside.
   b. silent.
   c. a piece of land.

Name_____ **Date** _____

Report Card Day

Read the paragraph. Then answer the questions.

Abby and Alice smiled and chattered as they walked home from school. They had received good report cards. Barney and Bill laughed as they tossed a football back and forth. Their report cards were good, too. As usual, Charley—who always got straight A's—was teasing Charlotte. But Charlotte didn't mind, because for once, her grades were just as good as Charley's. Dexter's grades were better than usual, and Jo and Ellen were happy with theirs. So were Gary and Fran, Helen and Ike, and Jonathan and Kitty. Zeke, however, looked rather glum. His report card was awful. Everyone had received good grades except Zeke.

1. Which sentence sums up the main idea of the paragraph? Underline it.

2. Which two students were tossing a football? _____

3. Who was teasing Charlotte? _____

4. Which of the following statements is probably true, based on the information in the paragraph? Circle your choice.

    a) Charley had never teased Charlotte before.

    b) Charley liked to tease Charlotte.

    c) Charlotte usually got better grades than Charley did.

5. Write a word that could have been used in place of the word *glum*. _____

Now use the word *glum* in a sentence of your own: _____

_____

_____

_____

Name_____ **Date** _____

Lobster Parade

Read the story. Then circle the correct answer to each question.

Lobsters have a hard outer shell made of many pieces joined together by thin, soft sections. Most lobsters have two large pinching claws on their front legs, but the *spiny lobster* has no claws. It gets its name from the spines which cover its shell.

Every winter, the spiny lobster <u>migrates</u> to warmer water. Using water currents to guide them, the lobsters move forward like a drill team, staying in formation by placing their front legs on the tail of the lobster ahead. Usually lobsters hide under rocks during the day and come out at night to feed. However, during migration time, they march night and day. They can cover as many as 50 miles in one week. Scientists think this single-file lobster parade across the ocean floor is due to the lobsters' attempt to escape cold winter water.

1. A good title for this story is
    a. Cold Winter Waters
    b. Marching Single-File
    c. The Spiny Lobster Migration

2. Spiny lobsters have
    a. four pinching claws.
    b. two pinching claws.
    c. no pinching claws.

3. During migration, the spiny lobster
    a. marches night and day.
    b. hides under rocks during the day.
    c. marches only at night.

4. Spiny lobsters probably do not live in
    a. Africa.
    b. Iceland.
    c. Bermuda.

5. The word *migrates* means
    a. moves from one area to another.
    b. shed its skin.
    c. marches in formation.

Name_____ **Date** _____

Life in Space

Read the paragraphs. Then answer the questions.

Do forms of life exist anywhere else in the universe other than Earth? Scientists have been examining this idea for many years. People have debated the possibility of life on other planets since at least the 5th century B.C. Scientists refer to this work as SETI, which means the "Search for Extraterrestrial (ex-tra-ter-res-tri-al) Intelligence." This work could tell us a lot about some distant world and its <u>inhabitants.</u>

Scientists use special equipment called radio telescopes. These telescopes do not see but rather listen for sounds of life beyond our world. Earth's own radio waves have now spread out more than 50 light years. or nearly 300 trillion miles. That means if creatures do exist in outer space, they could be listening to reruns of *I Dream of Jeannie!* Some day, scientists hope their special equipment will help them find proof that we are not alone in the universe.

1. Make up a new title that also expresses the main idea of the article.

   _____

2. For about how long have people debated the possibility of life on other planets?

   _____

3. What do scientists use to listen for sounds of life beyond our world?

   _____

4. (Circle your choice.) "Extraterrestrial Intelligence" probably refers to
   a. an extra long life.
   b. intelligent life on another planet.
   c. travel to another planet.

5. Find the word *inhabitants* in the article. Judging by the way it is used, give a brief definition of the word here. _____

   _____

Name_____ **Date** _____

Introducing Inference

Match the activities in column A to the items associated with them in column B.

	A		**B**
_____ 1.	playing tennis	a.	rope, pick, boots
_____ 2.	having a party	b.	a TV guide, chair, television
_____ 3.	telephoning	c.	basket, food, blanket
_____ 4.	building	d.	makeup, costume, applause
_____ 5.	painting	e.	racket, ball, net
_____ 6.	adding	f.	boat, wind, rope
_____ 7.	sailing	g.	pedals, pump, tires
_____ 8.	dancing	h.	music, friends, "munchies"
_____ 9.	watching TV	i.	gloves, sneakers, ring
_____ 10.	sleeping	j.	pencil, paper, numbers
_____ 11.	flying	k.	brush, canvas, easel
_____ 12.	mountain climbing	l.	dial tone, number, ring
_____ 13.	house cleaning	m.	soap, razor, mirror
_____ 14.	picnicking	n.	sheet, pillow, dark
_____ 15.	knitting	o.	music, movement, feet
_____ 16.	acting	p.	mop, broom, cleanser
_____ 17.	riding a horse	q.	needles, yarn, pattern
_____ 18.	boxing	r.	crane, brick, nails
_____ 19.	shaving	s.	plane, ticket, flight bag
_____ 20.	bicycling	t.	saddle, harness, hoof

Name_____ **Date** _____

Working with Inference

Match the activities in column A to the items associated with them in column B.

A

_____ 1.   bird-watching

_____ 2.   dating

_____ 3.   hiking

_____ 4.   writing

_____ 5.   camping

_____ 6.   playing football

_____ 7.   sewing

_____ 8.   reading

_____ 9.   cooking

_____10. traveling

_____11. farming

_____12. banking

_____13. driving

_____14. swimming

_____15. dining

_____16. jogging

_____17. gardening

_____18. singing

_____19. playing baseball

_____20. learning

B

a.   car, turn signal, road

b.   tent, bonfire, sleeping bag

c.   walking shoes, backpack, trail

d.   running shoes, stopwatch, warm-up

e.   pot, spoon, stove

f.   books, teachers, tests

g.   binoculars, birds, fields

h.   check, teller, balance

i.   plow, crops, barn

j.   movie, boyfriend, curfew

k.   ball, bat, home run

l.   appetizer, salad, dessert

m.   tune, microphone, harmony

n.   flower, mulch, bug spray

o.   pencil, paper, idea

p.   book, story, words

q.   field, helmet, goal post

r.   map, vacation, postcard

s.   pool, diving board, bathing suit

t.   needle, thread, thimble

Name_____ **Date** _____

Inference—A Review

Based on what you can infer from the following passage, answer the multiple choice questions. Write your answer on the blank provided.

There is a group of strong men riding in a truck. They arrive at a house. One of the men is older than the rest of them. He is dressed in a suit. The rest of the men are dressed in work clothes. The man in the suit rings the doorbell. A woman answers the front door. She is dressed in a uniform with an apron. She tells the man in the suit to wait a moment. Then another woman comes to the door. She is dressed in ordinary clothes. The man hands her a piece of paper which she signs. After that the other men go into the house and start covering the furniture in sheets and blankets. Then they carry the furniture out of the house and load it onto the back of the truck. When everything is in the truck, they drive over to a new house in another part of town and unload the furniture.

_____1. The men in the truck are
   a. ballet dancers   c. moving men
   b. movie stars   d. garbage collectors

_____2. The older man is
   a. a hairdresser   c. the supervisor
   b. The President of the d. one of the movers
       United States

_____3. The woman who first answers is
   a. the maid   c. a rock-and-roll singer
   b. the owner of the house d. a countess from France

_____4. The other woman who signs the paper is
   a. the maid   c. the owner of the house
   b. a neighbor   d. Barbra Streisand

_____5. They are moving the furniture because
   a. The house is on fire.
   b. The woman didn't pay her bills so the men are taking
       the furniture back to the store.
   c. The woman is moving to a new house.

Name_____ **Date** _____

Learning to Draw Conclusions

For each situation stated below, draw a conclusion by circling the most likely explanation.

1. The car stalled three times.
    a. It's summertime.
    b. It needs painting.
    c. It needs servicing.

2. It was still dark when John awoke.
    a. John is lazy.
    b. It is very early.
    c. John will be late for school.

3. She heard a large crash when the box dropped.
    a. She dropped the box in some water.
    b. The box contained a present.
    c. The contents were breakable.

4. When he drove up, his father was standing angrily by the door.
    a. He was late getting home.
    b. He had been to a basketball game.
    c. He dropped his date off first.

5. They all cheered when the final buzzer rang.
    a. They liked the sound of the buzzer.
    b. They lost the game.
    c. They won the game.

6. She said, "ouch," and then noticed she had stuck her finger with the needle.
    a. She was sewing.
    b. She was washing the dishes.
    c. She was dancing.

7. Frank was happy and couldn't wait to get home.
    a. He had flunked algebra.
    b. He had a good report card.
    c. He had been late for school that morning.

8. He looked down and watched as the trees seemed to grow smaller and smaller.
    a. He was falling asleep.
    b. He was flying in a plane.
    c. He was driving to work.

Name_____ **Date** _____

Drawing Conclusions

For each situation stated below, draw a conclusion by circling the most likely explanation.

1. For the first time in months, Hillary heard a bird singing outside.
   a. Her window was open.
   b. She was tired of the radio.
   c. Spring was coming.

2. Jake sipped the steaming liquid, hoping it would keep him awake.
   a. He was drinking hot milk.
   b. He was drinking coffee.
   c. He was drinking iced tea.

3. At this height there were no trees, and they could see for miles.
   a. They were riding in a hot-air balloon.
   b. They were in a car.
   c. They were on a boat.

4. She cried as her parents drove away, and she looked at her unfamiliar new dorm room.
   a. She hated the room.
   b. Her feet hurt.
   c. She was getting homesick.

5. He took aim and fired his spear gun at the large barracuda.
   a. He was in a sporting goods store.
   b. He was swimming in the pool.
   c. He was scuba diving.

6. He had never seen so many books before.
   a. He was in a restaurant.
   b. He was in his house.
   c. He was in a very large library.

7. She whispered the code word to the dark figure in the hall.
   a. She was buying a pair of shoes.
   b. She was a spy.
   c. She was a salesperson.

8. He flew through the air, did a flip, and then fell into the net.
   a. He was a diving champion.
   b. He was a trapeze artist.
   c. He was a mountain climber.

Name_____ Date _____

Practice Drawing Conclusions

For each situation stated below, draw a conclusion by circling the most likely explanation.

1. The bread was hard as a rock.
    a. It was baked with lots of iron.
    b. It was stale.
    c. It wasn't really bread.

2. Suddenly, every light in town went out.
    a. Everyone was going to bed at the same time.
    b. No one had paid the light bill.
    c. There was a power failure.

3. As Inez hurried home in her car, she saw a flashing light behind her and heard a siren.
    a. Inez lived in a police station.
    b. She had been speeding.
    c. She was seeing things.

4. All the people at the movie began to scream and cover their eyes.
    a. It was a horror movie.
    b. It was a comedy.
    c. It was boring.

5. He knocked and knocked, but no one answered.
    a. He didn't knock hard enough.
    b. No one was home.
    c. He should have used the doorbell.

6. When he got home, he noticed that everyone had coats on as they sat close to the fireplace.
    a. His family was in the coat business.
    b. The heat had gone off.
    c. They were playing a trick on him.

7. When he finished, everyone laughed for about five minutes.
    a. He told them his name.
    b. He asked for a glass of water.
    c. He told them a joke.

8. As she made the salad, her eyes began to water.
    a. She hated making salad.
    b. She was peeling onions.
    c. She cut herself.

Name_____ **Date** _____

Reviewing Inference & Drawing Conclusions

Read the statements below. Then write the name of the job or profession of the person who would most likely make the statement. The first one is done for you.

1. "Blue chip stocks are a sure bet." stockbroker

2. "Your grocery bill comes to $40.58." _____

3. "Looks like you need a new muffler." _____

4. "My client is not guilty." _____

5. "I design each house individually." _____

6. "I'm going to have to operate." _____

7. "How do you want your steak?" _____

8. "The math test will be given next week." _____

9. "You'll have no more trouble with your sink." _____

10. "I typed all the letters." _____

11. "Take your medication, Mr. Jones." _____

12. "If elected, I will be honest." _____

13. "I'll have to pull that tooth." _____

14. "This life insurance policy will give you peace of mind." _____

15. "Good evening. This is the six o'clock news." _____

16. "I've finished installing your new light switch." _____

17. "Do you realize how fast you were driving?" _____

18. "I'm sure we have dresses in your size." _____

19. "It will be cloudy today, with a 60% chance of rain." _____

Name_____ **Date** _____

49

Inference & Drawing Conclusions—A Review

Read the paragraphs below. Use inference skills to draw conclusions based on the paragraphs. Circle either "true" or "false" after each statement.

Mary's stomach growled as she asked Frank to get her some popcorn. Frank said she would have to wait until intermission. To make matters worse, Mary had left her glasses at home. A few minutes later, there was a boring scene on the screen, so Mary decided to get some popcorn herself. She discovered that her shoe was stuck on some bubble gum and other garbage on the floor. Frank laughed.

1. Mary is hungry.   TRUE or FALSE

2. Frank and Mary are at Mary's house.   TRUE or FALSE

3. Frank and Mary are at a movie theater.   TRUE or FALSE

4. Mary can see the picture very clearly.   TRUE or FALSE

5. The theater is kept very clean.   TRUE or FALSE

6. Mary is having a wonderful time.   TRUE or FALSE

There is a large crowd of people standing around. Everyone is dressed in light colors and fabrics. The girls are wearing thin cotton dresses or shorts. Some people are wearing sandals. In the background there are lots of trees. Behind the trees are tall buildings. Many people are either squinting or wearing sunglasses. Most of them are either singing or humming as they listen to the music.

1. It is a cold and rainy day.   TRUE or FALSE

2. The above scene takes place in an auditorium.   TRUE or FALSE

3. It is warm outside.   TRUE or FALSE

4. The sun is hidden by clouds.   TRUE or FALSE

5. The people are in a park in a city.   TRUE or FALSE

6. The story takes place in the 1500's.   TRUE or FALSE

7. It is an outdoor concert.   TRUE or FALSE

Name_____ Date _____

Matching Cause & Effect

Make the *best* match between the causes in column A and their possible effects in column B.

A. Causes

_____ 1. fire

_____ 2. broken alarm clock

_____ 3. high mileage

_____ 4. ignoring a red light

_____ 5. employment

_____ 6. sunbathing

_____ 7. boiling water

_____ 8. stop sign

_____ 9. tight shoes

_____10. overdue book

_____11. too little sleep

_____12. skipped meal

_____13. lit dynamite

_____14. electric current

_____15. vacuuming

B. Effects

a. shock

b. salary

c. aching feet

d. worn-out tires

e. clean rug

f. smoke

g. explosion

h. late for school

i. hunger

j. steam

k. traffic ticket

l. tan

m. stopped car

n. library fine

o. sleepiness

Name_____ **Date** _____

51

Signal Words—Cause & Effect

Certain words and phrases give us the signal that we are reading a "cause and effect" statement. Study the "signal" words and phrases listed in the box. Then, circle the signal words or phrases in the sentences below.

consequently	so that	as a result
because	if/then	since
in order that	has caused	resulted in

1. If the train departs on time, then we will be on time for the bus.

2. He put all his money into a special account so that it would earn the highest possible interest.

3. He lost his watch because the strap was loose and frayed.

4. She was late for work almost every day; consequently, she lost her job.

5. Since you won't tell me what I want to know, I'll find out from someone else.

6. He stayed late in order that others could leave early.

7. His dedication and hard work resulted in his promotion to president of the company.

8. Many people claim that inflation has caused most of the nation's economic woes.

9. Over the years the steady rain has caused the rock to wear away.

10. Since she was so late, the judge fined her $20.

Name_____ **Date** _____

Cause & Effect Statements

Certain words and phrases give us the signal that we are reading a "cause and effect" statement. Study the "signal" words and phrases listed in the box. Then, circle the signal words or phrases in the sentences below.

consequently	so that	as a result
because	if/then	since
in order that	has caused	resulted in

1. The train derailed because a section of track was missing.

2. In order that no one else would get hurt, he covered the wires with tape.

3. The lights were turned off in the store so that the shoppers would realize it was closed.

4. The double tackle he received in the football game resulted in torn cartilage in his knee.

5. The rug was ruined because grape juice was spilled on it.

6. He knew that the train would leave at 12:00; consequently, he made sure to be at the station by 11:50.

7. The house burned down because an electrical outlet was overloaded.

8. If you leave a cake in the oven too long, then it will burn.

9. Because the patient went to his dentist twice a year, he had good teeth.

10. As a result of her high grades, she won a full scholarship to college.

Name_____ **Date** _____

Finding the Cause

In each sentence below, circle the cause. The cause explains the "why."

1. Because televisions were so expensive at first, many people could not afford to buy one.

2. Millions of people bought televisions in the 1950's because they were so exciting.

3. Movies became less popular since people could watch TV at home.

4. People go to the doctor when they get sick.

5. Medicine is a highly skilled practice, so doctors are often expensive.

6. If you need an operation you will probably have to go to the hospital.

7. Most people buy health insurance because hospitals are so expensive.

8. Because most people get sick at some time, it's important to have health insurance.

9. During World War II, many countries suffered heavy losses because of aerial bombing.

10. As you grow older your bones get more brittle.

Name_____ Date _____

Locating Cause & Effect

Read the sentences below and the phrases that follow. Place a "C" after the phrase if it is a *cause* (why), and an "E" if it is an *effect* (what).

1. There is life on the earth because we are the right distance from the sun's heat.

_____life on the earth
_____right distance from the sun's heat

2. If we were too close to the sun, then it would be too hot for plants to grow.

_____too close to the sun
_____too hot for plants to grow

3. Because Mercury does not spin, one side of it is very hot.

_____Mercury does not spin.
_____One side of it is very hot.

4. Jupiter does not have life on it because its atmosphere consists of poisonous gases.

_____Jupiter does not have life on it.
_____Its atmosphere consists of poisonous gases.

5. The outer planets, Pluto and Neptune, are frozen because they are so far from the sun.

_____Pluto and Neptune are frozen.
_____They are so far from the sun.

6. Because Pluto and Neptune are so cold, they probably cannot support life.

_____Pluto and Neptune are so cold.
_____They probably cannot support life.

Name_____ **Date** _____

Cause & Effect in a Passage

Read the passage, then answer the questions.

Many people like football because it means making so many decisions all the time. Football is like chess because in both games the players stop after each move (play) to decide on the next one.

Others like football because it is a contact sport. The rough action on the field is exciting because it tests the players as few other sports can.

Lots of people like football because it is colorful. Exciting marching bands make half time fun to watch.

Fill in the missing causes:

1. People like football because:

    a. _____

    b. _____

    c. _____

2. Football is like chess because:

    _____

In each sentence underline the *effect* and circle the *cause*:

3. Football is popular because there are so many reasons for liking it.

4. Half times are popular because marching bands are fun to watch.

5. The rough action of football is exciting because it tests the players.

Finding Cause & Effect

Read the passage. Then, in the sentences below, circle the *cause* and underline the *effect*.

Because planes are so fast, people can now cross the United States in about five hours. Traveling is faster because a plane can fly at about 600 miles per hour. Before the jet age it would take about three days in a train to cross the country. Because people can get to places so fast, they can go longer distances on their vacations. For example, if a person had a week's vacation and had to take the train across the country, then he or she would only have time for a quick tour of the train station before the return trip.

Planes themselves have been getting faster all the time as a result of advancing technology. A propeller plane would take about 12 or 13 hours to cross the Atlantic Ocean. A jet can cross it in about seven hours. Now people can go from New York to Paris in approximately 3½ hours because of the supersonic Concorde.

1. Because planes are so fast, people can now cross the United States in about five hours.

2. Traveling is faster than ever today because a plane can fly at about 600 miles per hour.

3. Because people can get to places so fast, they can go longer distances on their vacations.

4. Planes themselves have been getting faster all the time as a result of advancing technology.

5. Now people can go from New York to Paris in about 3½ hours because of the supersonic Concorde.

Name_____ **Date** _____

Fact & Opinion

Each sentence below states either a fact or an opinion. Read each sentence, then circle the correct answer. The first one is done for you.

1. Daylight in the summer lasts longer than daylight in the winter.

    (FACT)　　　　　　　　　OPINION

2. Absence makes the heart grow fonder.

    FACT　　　　　　　　　OPINION

3. America put the first man on the moon.

    FACT　　　　　　　　　OPINION

4. The Grand Canyon is the most beautiful place on Earth.

    FACT　　　　　　　　　OPINION

5. The moon is a satellite of the earth.

    FACT　　　　　　　　　OPINION

6. The full moon is very romantic.

    FACT　　　　　　　　　OPINION

7. Billboards ruin the beauty of a highway.

    FACT　　　　　　　　　OPINION

8. John Wayne starred in many movies.

    FACT　　　　　　　　　OPINION

9. John Wayne was the greatest actor who ever lived.

    FACT　　　　　　　　　OPINION

10. Swamps are unpleasant places.

    FACT　　　　　　　　　OPINION

11. George Washington was America's first President.

    FACT　　　　　　　　　OPINION

12. George Washington never told a lie.

    FACT　　　　　　　　　OPINION

13. There are twelve months in a calendar year.

    FACT　　　　　　　　　OPINION

14. A person's character is determined by his or her sun sign.

    FACT　　　　　　　　　OPINION

15. Most people spend too much time watching television.

    FACT　　　　　　　　　OPINION

Name_____ **Date** _____

Distinguishing Fact from Opinion

Each sentence below states either a fact or an opinion. Read each sentence, then circle the correct answer. The first one is done for you.

1. Bananas are one of the most delicious fruits.

   FACT   (OPINION)

2. Sugar is bad for your teeth.

   FACT   OPINION

3. Coffee tastes better than tea.

   FACT   OPINION

4. New York is the greatest city in the United States.

   FACT   OPINION

5. Plants make a home beautiful.

   FACT   OPINION

6. Coffee is made from beans.

   FACT   OPINION

7. New York is a noisy city.

   FACT   OPINION

8. President Lincoln freed the slaves in 1863.

   FACT   OPINION

9. Tulips are the prettiest flowers.

   FACT   OPINION

10. The earth is the third planet from the sun.

   FACT   OPINION

11. House plants will die without water.

   FACT   OPINION

12. Alexander Graham Bell invented the telephone.

   FACT   OPINION

13. Dogs make better pets than goldfish.

   FACT   OPINION

14. Lizards and snakes both belong to the reptile family.

   FACT   OPINION

15. Silver dollars are the prettiest coins.

   FACT   OPINION

Name_____ **Date** _____

Fact & Opinion Game

Read the sentences below. Each square in the Tic-Tac-Toe board has a number that corresponds to each sentence below. Put an "X" in the box if the sentence is a fact, put an "O" in the box if the sentence is an opinion. If you are right, you will be a winner at Tic-Tac-Toe.

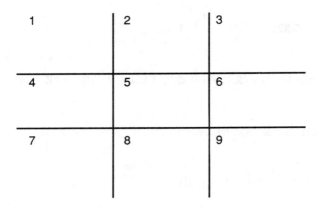

Fact = X   Opinion = O

1. Skydiving requires a parachute.

2. Many of his fans called Elvis Presley "The King."

3. "Real Farms" cookies taste best because they are cooked slowly.

4. Nobody really knows what caused the dinosaurs to vanish from the earth.

5. In the United States, all registered voters have a right to cast a ballot in the Presidential election.

6. Niagara Falls is the best place to go on a honeymoon.

7. The safest place to keep money is under a mattress.

8. It's a good idea to read every best-selling novel that comes along.

9. Many people lost their jobs during the Great Depression.

Name_____ Date _____

Fun with Fact & Opinion

Read the sentences below. Each square in the Tic-Tac-Toe board has a number that corresponds to each sentence below. Put an "X" in the box if the sentence is a fact, put an "O" in the box if the sentence is an opinion. If you are right, you will be a winnter at Tic-Tac-Toe.

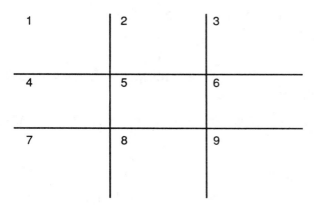

Fact = X   Opinion = O

1. Saturday is the best day of the week.

2. Most months of the year have 31 days.

3. In American football, a touchdown is worth six points.

4. Freedom of speech is the most important item in the Bill of Rights.

5. Good mileage is the most important consideration when buying a new car.

6. Freedom of speech is guaranteed by the First Amendment.

7. Although other parties exist, American politics is dominated by the two-party system.

8. The two-party system is the most efficient way to conduct elections.

9. Abraham Lincoln was the first Republican President.

Name_____ **Date** _____

Choosing the Facts

Each exercise below contains two sentences. One is a fact, the other is an opinion. Write an "F" next to the sentence that states a *fact*. The first one is done for you.

1. __F__Astronomers use large radio telescopes to chart distant stars.

   _____Astronomy is a fascinating and informative subject.

2. _____Some college libraries are replacing the Dewey decimal system with the Library of Congress system.

   _____The Library of Congress system is more efficient than the Dewey decimal system.

3. _____Julius Caesar is considered by many historians to be the first dictator.

   _____Julius Caesar is one of the most wicked men the world has ever known.

4. _____The new city tax proposal will increase property taxes by 13 percent.

   _____The new city tax proposal will make our town a better place to live.

5. _____"Moppo" is amazing! It will clean anything!

   _____"Moppo" contains a grease remover.

6. _____About 20 people attended Mrs. Watson's surprise party.

   _____Everyone had a wonderful time at Mrs. Watson's party.

7. _____Oil is the world's most important energy source.

   _____Oil prices play an important role in the economy of many nations.

8. _____Football is a dangerous and violent sport.

   _____Football is played on a 100-yard-long field.

9. _____The American Declaration of Independence is one of the most important statements in the world.

   _____The Declaration of Independence helped to shape the course of the new American nation.

Name_____ Date _____

Recognizing an Opinion

Each exercise below contains two sentences. One is a fact, the other is an opinion. Write an "O" next to the sentence that states an *opinion*. The first one is done for you.

1. __O__ Owning a car is a lot of trouble and worry.

   _____ Most states require you to have insurance if you own a car.

2. _____ Saturn is the most striking and beautiful planet in the solar system.

   _____ One of the unique features of the planet Saturn is that it has visible rings.

3. _____ The World Series is held in the fall.

   _____ The Super Bowl is more exciting than the World Series.

4. _____ The Civil War was a turbulent and violent period of American history.

   _____ The Civil War is the most interesting period of American history.

5. _____ William Shakespeare is unquestionably the greatest playwright who ever lived.

   _____ Some of Shakespeare's most famous plays are *Hamlet*, *A Midsummer Night's Dream*, and *Macbeth*.

6. _____ There are many more laborsaving inventions today than there were a century ago.

   _____ Life is much more pleasant today than it was a century ago.

7. _____ Clothes made out of "natural" fibers like cotton are better than clothes made out of synthetic fibers like polyester.

   _____ Some people buy clothes made with polyester because they are durable and easy to care for.

8. _____ You should never go on a trip without taking traveler's checks.

   _____ An advantage of traveler's checks is that if they are lost or stolen, they can be easily replaced.

Name_____ **Date** _____

Finding the Fact

Each exercise below contains two sentences. One is a fact, the other is an opinion. Underline the sentence that states a *fact*.

1. Jack beat the socks off the other racers.
   Jack won the race by 30 seconds.

2. Joe's car has many luxurious features.
   Joe's car cost 100 dollars more than the others.

3. The president won the election by a landslide.
   The president won 51% of the votes.

4. Only people over 30 can be successful in retail sales.
   People of all ages work in retail sales.

5. Pets are a nuisance to feed and care for.
   Many people enjoy owning pets.

6. The criminal justice system is in sad shape.
   Many of the nation's prisons are overcrowded.

7. Computers can do calculations in much less time than human beings.
   The advent of the computer has improved the world.

8. Natural gas is much better for home heating than oil.
   Because of its lower cost, many families switched to natural gas in the 1970's.

Name_____ Date _____

Locating Fact & Opinion

Read each passage. Then write an "F" beside the number of the sentence that states a *fact* and an "O" beside the number of the sentence that states an *opinion*.

1. Zoos are a great place to visit because you can have fun and learn things at the same time.   2. Zoos contain many kinds of animals.   3. There are usually mammals, reptiles, amphibians, and birds.   4. Some zoos have insect displays as well.   5. The big cats, such as the lions, tigers, and leopards, are beautiful.   6. But elephants are friendlier to humans.   7. Like elephants, rhinos and hippos come from Africa.   8. There, many of these animals still live in the wild.   9. Many of the wild animals in the U.S. live in national parks. 10. Here they can live in the wild, yet they are protected from hunters by the government.

1.____   2.____   3.____   4.____   5.____   6.____   7.____   8.____   9.____   10.____

1. Food is needed for growth and health.   2. Not everyone eats right, however.   3. A balanced diet consists of meat and fish, dairy products, vegetables and fruit, as well as starches.   4. Each of the four food groups contains certain nutrients we need. 5. Vitamin C is in oranges.   6. Oranges are delicious.   7. Some people don't eat meat, a valuable source of protein, but protein is also available from peanuts and soy beans.   8. Vitamin D is essential to health.   9. Vitamin D is found in milk and cheese. 10. Many nutritious foods are not enjoyable.

1.____   2.____   3.____   4.____   5.____   6.____   7.____   8.____   9.____   10.____

Name_____   Date _____

Reading a Graph—Fact & Opinion

Look at the graph, then read the sentences below. Some of the sentences are facts taken from the graph; some of the sentences are opinions about the graph. Write "F" beside the *facts* from the graph, and "O" beside the *opinions*.

The Popularity of Two Fast Foods: Hamburgers and Fried Chicken

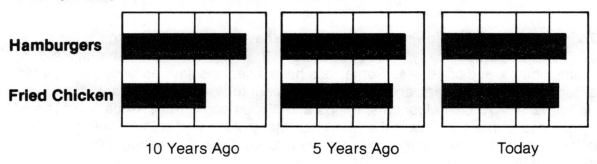

Hamburgers

Fried Chicken

10 Years Ago   5 Years Ago   Today

1. _____ Ten years ago, hamburgers were more popular than fried chicken.

2. _____ Five years ago, chicken was almost as popular as hamburgers.

3. _____ As you can see, hamburgers are better for you than chicken.

4. _____ People who sold hamburgers made more money than people who sold fried chicken.

5. _____ Today, although hamburgers are still more popular, fried chicken is almost as popular.

6. _____ Fried chicken tastes better than hamburgers.

7. _____ Hamburger is cheaper than fried chicken.

8. _____ If you were smart, you would take advantage of the growing popularity of chicken and open a chicken restaurant.

9. _____ It's obvious that some day soon, fried chicken will be more popular than hamburger.

10. _____ In the last ten years, hamburgers have always been more popular than chicken.

Name_____ **Date** _____

Separating Fact From Opinion

Read the travel ad and see if you can separate the facts from the opinions. Then, in the blanks provided, write an "O" beside the *opinions,* and and "F" beside the *facts.*

This will be your dream vacation! Exotic Travel is proud to announce our El Cheapo Dream Come True First-Class Vacation Wonder! From the moment you climb on board our commuter airline, until you touch down in El Paso, you'll be pampered by our experienced staff. You'll see seven cities! You'll have the time of your life!

You'll spend seven days in Mexico. You'll taste Mexican food as only those who know how can cook it. You'll see the ruins of Montezuma's empire. You'll visit Acapulco! You'll be able to gamble in its casinos.

You'll enjoy fun-filled days in Mexico. Then, you'll tour the cities of America's Southwest. You'll see the Astrodome, and get free tickets for a baseball game there.

The trip lasts fourteen days, all accommodations and one meal each day included. And the cost? Only $700 per person (for double occupancy).

This will be your dream vacation! _____
You climb on board our commuter airline. _____
You touch down in El Paso. _____
You'll be pampered by our experienced staff. _____
You'll see seven cities! _____
You'll have the time of your life! _____
You'll spend seven days in Mexico. _____
You'll see the ruins of Montezuma's empire. _____
You'll visit Acapulco! _____
You'll be able to gamble in its casinos. _____
You'll enjoy seven fun-filled days in Mexico. _____
You'll tour the cities of America's Southwest. _____
You'll see the Astrodome. _____
You'll get free tickets for a baseball game there. _____
The trip lasts fourteen days. _____
All accommodations and one meal each day included. _____

Name_____ Date _____

Is It Fact or Opinion?

Read the passage and see if you can separate the facts from the opinions. Then, in the blanks provided, write an "O" beside the *opinions,* and and "F" beside the *facts.*

HORRIBLE MONSTERS FROM OUTER SPACE is a terrific movie! It has action, monsters, and outer space! You'll love it! I was glued to my seat, except, of course, for the times when I jumped right out of it.

It begins when a giant asteroid collides with the moon and sends a shower of little green slimy droplets raining on the earth. At first, everyone is just inconvenienced trying to clean up the mess, but soon the little droplets start to grow wings. They turn into fabulously scary creatures! They get bigger and bigger. Soon, each is bigger than two World Trade Centers stacked on top of each other!

Giles Goodbody gives the best performance of his career, and Sandra Mayday is outrageous as the jaunty reporter who falls in love with the leader of the horrible monsters from outer space.

You'll love it! _____
HORRIBLE MONSTERS FROM OUTER SPACE is a terrific movie! _____
It has action, monsters, and outer space! _____
You'll love it! _____
It begins when a giant asteroid collides with the moon. _____
A shower of little green slimy droplets rains on the earth. _____
At first, everyone is just inconvenienced. _____
But soon the droplets start to grow wings. _____
They turn into fabulously scary creatures! _____
They get bigger and bigger. _____
Giles Goodbody gives the best performance of his career. _____
Sandra Mayday is outrageous. _____
She falls in love with the leader of the
    horrible monsters from outer space. _____

Name_____ Date _____

68

Understanding Tone

Tone is the result of the author's attitude. The author's attitude might be negative or positive. An author will often use figurative language (words that tell a story or paint a picture) to express tone. Study the following sentences. First, underline the figurative language. Next, in the blank provided, put a plus sign (+) if the phrase expresses a positive attitude, a minus sign (–) if the phrase expresses a negative attitude. The first one is done for you.

____ —_____ 1. He's a <u>bull in a china shop</u>.

_____ 2. His mind is like a sieve.

_____ 3. He was a finely-tuned running machine in the marathon.

_____ 4. She was always the fly in the ointment.

_____ 5. His ideas are as good as a screen door in a submarine.

_____ 6. Her arrival was like the light at the end of the tunnel.

_____ 7. She came out of the troublesome situation smelling like a rose.

_____ 8. Some people are always thorns in your side.

_____ 9. He was a prince to us.

_____ 10. She paces the room like a caged animal.

_____ 11. Clara Barton was a beacon of virtue.

_____ 12. He is a ringmaster at business meetings.

_____ 13. He acted as silly as a clown.

_____ 14. Her mind was a treasure-trove of imaginative thoughts.

_____ 15. She was as poor as a church mouse.

Name_____ Date _____

Working with Tone

Tone is the result of the author's attitude. The author's attitude might be negative or positive. An author will often use figurative language (words that tell a story or paint a picture) to express tone. Study the following sentences. First, underline the figurative language. Next, in the blank provided, put a plus sign (+) if the phrase expresses a positive attitude, a minus sign (–) if the phrase expresses a negative attitude. The first one is done for you.

_____+_____ 1. I bought the painting <u>for a song</u>.

_____ 2. His memory is like a computer.

_____ 3. Her nails are as sharp as cat claws.

_____ 4. His face is as expressionless as a mask.

_____ 5. He is a snake in the grass.

_____ 6. She floated into the hotel like a spring breeze.

_____ 7. He was a tiger on the pitcher's mound.

_____ 8. She behaved like an angel.

_____ 9. John is as thin as a stick.

_____ 10. The girl's eyes were glittering stars.

_____ 11. His mind worked with the precision of a clock.

_____ 12. The critic's cutting remarks tore the play to shreds.

_____ 13. Her tongue is razor-sharp.

_____ 14. Barbra Streisand's voice is like a bell.

_____ 15. Her date was as exciting as a wet dishrag.

Name_____ Date _____

Tone—Judgment Words

Judgment words are clues to an author's feelings or judgments about his or her subject. For example, words such as "ridiculous," "silly," and "outdated" express dislike. Read each passage below. Circle all the judgment words or phrases. Then, answer the question about the writer's attitude. (There may be more than one correct answer.)

The Frightened Duck, Mayfield's newest restaurant, is a delightful addition to the dining scene. The duck they serve is superb. What's more, they serve the French delicacy, "pressed duck." I found the service to be slow. But be patient and be prepared. When you get the bill it won't be cheap. But if you love food and are willing to pay for it, then you can't do better than at The Frightened Duck.

The writer's attitude is one of:

A. sarcasm   C. praise

B. dislike   D. indifference

Last night I dined at Mayfield's newest rip-off joint, the Frightened Duck. Maybe on special occasions I would be willing to pay $100 for two, but the food and service had better be exceptional. They aren't. Even the famous "pressed duck" tasted more like it came from a dry cleaner's than a kitchen. And the service took so long. Remember, don't say I didn't warn you.

The writer's attitude is one of:

A. sarcasm   C. praise

B. dislike   D. indifference

Name_____ **Date** _____

Tone—A Review

In each passage below, underline the judgment words or phrases. Then, in the space provided, describe the author's tone in your own words.

Cab driving in New York City is a great job. You meet all kinds of people. Most people are fun and interesting. Very few of them are dishonest.

As a cab driver, you also get to know all the different parts of the city. There's the beautiful East Side, the unusual Chinatown, or the exciting Greenwich Village, All in all, cab driving can be a very rewarding experience.

The author's tone is one of _____

_____

_____

Las Vegas is one of the most popular vacation spots in America. The hotels have great performers. The hotels themselves are quite spectacular, with luxurious lobbies and spacious rooms.

The author's tone is one of _____

_____

_____

When my car broke down in Claggsville, I thought the calm, relaxed pace of a small town might be a pleasant change. I was wrong. Of all the one-horse towns in America, Claggsville must qualify for some kind of prize. The restaurants, all two of them, serve dreary food. The one theater shows five-year-old movies. Even the people of Claggsville are boring.

The author's tone is one of _____

_____

_____

Time to Review

Read the passage, then write the letter of the correct answer on the blanks provided.

Camp Windy Wood, in the heart of scenic North Carolina, is a marvelous camp for children aged 8 to 14. Situated next to a crystal lake on 300 acres of rolling woodland, this camp is able to offer a varied range of opportunities for recreation. Horseback riding, archery, swimming, boating, hiking, and crafts (including pottery and woodworking) are among the activities available. Items from Camp Windy Wood workshops have won many prizes at craft fairs and local exhibitions.

1. Read these statements from the above passage. Write "O" beside the opinions. "F" beside the facts.

_____ "Camp Windy Wood...is a marvelous summer camp."

_____ "Camp Windy Wood...is for children aged 8 to 14."

_____ "Camp Windy Wood offers archery and swimming."

_____ "North Carolina is scenic."

_____ 2. Based on the passage above, since the camp is situated beside a lake among woodlands, the camp

    a. has a lot of mosquitoes.

    b. is a dangerous place.

    c. can offer many kinds of recreation.

    d. wins prizes at crafts fairs.

_____ 3. You can infer from a careful reading of the passage that Camp Windy Wood seems to excel in

    a. archery.

    b. crafts.

    c. horseback riding.

    d. water sports.

_____ 4. Draw a conclusion from the information presented in the passage. The best time to go to Camp Windy Wood is

    a. spring.

    b. summer.

    c. autumn.

    d. winter.

_____ 5. In the passage above, circle the judgment words or phrases, then choose the answer below that best describes the tone of the passage.

    a. enthusiasm

    b. indifference

    c. dislike

    d. criticism

Name_____ **Date** _____

Overall Review

Read the passage, then write the letter of the correct answer on the blanks provided.

The Morrisville Community Theater's production of the *Pirates of Penzance* is absolutely delightful. My daughter, who plays the female lead, sings like a nightingale and is as graceful as a gazelle.

The play begins as a young man decides to give up piracy, against the wishes of his fellow pirates. By the end of the play, eight other pirates give up their lives of crime in order to marry the eight daughters of the Major General.

There are some problems with the production, however. Some of the actresses playing the Major General's daughters, as well as some of the actors playing the pirates, need to take voice lessons, as they hit an occasional sour note. But, the dancing is flawless, and the audience laughed throughout. Don't miss this enjoyable play.

1. Read these statements from the above passage. Write "O" beside the opinions. "F" beside the facts.

_____ "The production…is…delightful."

_____ "My daughter…sings like a nightingale."

_____ "A young man…gives up piracy."

_____ "Eight pirates…marry the eight daughters of the Major General."

2. Write "C" before the cause and "E" before the effect.

_____ The pirates give up their lives of crime.

_____ The pirates marry the eight daughters of the Major General.

_____ 3. You can infer from the passage above that the audience

    a. was bored by the play.   c. enjoyed the play.

    b. disliked the play.   d. was indifferent to the play.

_____ 4. Draw a conclusion from the information presented in the passage. *The Pirates of Penzance* appears to be primarily

    a. a tragedy.   c. a drama.

    b. an historical play.   d. a comedy.

_____ 5. In the passage above, underline the judgment words or phrases, then choose the answer below that best describes the tone of the passage.

    a. enthusiasm mixed with criticism   c. criticism

    b. enthusiasm   d. indifference

Name_____ **Date** _____